COMPLETE BOOK
OF DRILLS
FOR WINNING SOCCER

COMPLETE BOOK
OF DRILLS
FOR WINNING SOCCER

James P. McGettigan

PARKER PUBLISHING COMPANY
West Nyack, New York 10994

Library of Congress Cataloging-in-Publication Data

McGettigan, James P.
    Complete book of drills for winning soccer.
        p. cm.
    Includes index.
    ISBN 0-13-156356-4
    1. Soccer—Training. I. Title.
    GV943.9.T7M32 1980   80-15783
    796.334'2   CIP

Printed in the United States of America

20   19   18   17   16   15   14

ISBN 0-13-156356-4

PARKER PUBLISHING COMPANY
West Nyack, NY 10994

A Simon & Schuster Company

On the World Wide Web at http://www.phdirect.com

Prentice-Hall International (UK) Limited, *London*
Prentice-Hall of Australia Pty. Limited, *Sydney*
Prentice-Hall Canada Inc., *Toronto*
Prentice-Hall Hispanoamericana, S.A., *Mexico*
Prentice-Hall of India Private Limited, *New Delhi*
Prentice-Hall of Japan, Inc., *Tokyo*
Simon & Schuster Asia Pte. Ltd., *Singapore*
Editora Prentice-Hall do Brasil, Ltda., *Rio de Janeiro*

Dedication

**To my four children
Eve, Joe, Sarah and Jamie
and to
Andy Eisele**

How to Get the Most From This Book

This is a book of soccer drills for you and your players. These drills are a means to an end—the end being coordinated, organized team play.

Traditionally, soccer books are divided into three areas: technique, tactics and physical fitness. Since these categories are interrelated, I have avoided using the same classifications in structuring this book. For the sake of clarity and expedience, the chapters are divided according to the desired major objective of the drills and games.

There are four sections:

1. Skill Drills
2. Basic Patterns
3. Special Situations
4. Training

Skill drills are for acquiring a specific skill, such as heading, passing, trapping, etc.

Basic patterns involve small groups of players, with the players' final objective being to move a ball toward a goal.

Special situations are drills and set plays for special situations that occur during a game, such as: kickoff plays, corner kicks, corner crossing plays, throw-in plays and penalty kicks.

The training section includes training games, individual training activities with a ball and without a ball. Training games are games that emphasize practice in various techniques and tactics normally overlooked unless specifically planned for and included in practice sessions. An example would be playing soccer with a weak foot, which would force the player to participate in an exercise specifically designed to strengthen his foot.

The individual training activities concentrate on what an individual can do to prepare physically for playing the game of soccer. This section also includes physical conditioning exercises with and without the ball.

Soccer is a team sport, yet each individual bears a responsibility for using his individual technical skills for the benefit of the entire team through direct interaction among two, three or four players in the immediate area of the ball.

It is impractical for you to give direct instruction to the entire team since this type of instruction is too time consuming. It causes a situation in which most of the players stand around while a few players receive instructions. Consequently, it is better to break your team into smaller groups in order to increase the frequency of interaction. In small drill groups, the players can understand the purpose of maneuvers and visualize what is being demonstrated.

Although individual technique and organic fitness can occur concomitantly in practice sessions directed toward team and group tactics, it is necessary to set specific practice-schedule time aside for improving players' potential in these areas of preparation. Therefore, certain sections of this book have been devoted to activities and drills to improve organic fitness and individual technique. A variety of these activities at your fingertips will help to get the most from your players and prevent boredom.

It is not necessary that you use all of the drills in this book; you can pick out only the drills that meet your needs. If you want, you can try all of the drills and choose the ones you think are accomplishing your purpose or objective. For example, you may notice that during match play, your players are consistently losing the ball because they are forcing the play rather than pulling the defense out and getting behind it. By looking through this book, you will find a drill that will help your team accommodate its lack of width and improvization in match play. Practice sessions with a variety of drills from Chapter 9 (Small Group Passing Drills) and a selected number of Corner Crossing Drills from Chapter 10, you should be able to alleviate your problem of forcing a ball. By encouraging diagonal runs, back passing, decoy runs, place changing, quick switching and other diversionary tactics, you help your team vary its attack and eliminate "the straight line to the goal" approach. Each of these diversionary tactics are explained in the beginning of Chapter 9. Thus, during a practice session, you can drill to improve your team's problems of forcing the play.

Many of the drills in this book may not be new to you, but you can use this book as a reference source or as a supplementary aid.

The drills for this book come from many sources: players, coaches, magazines, books, movies, clinics and other sources. Many of the drills will be used frequently, while others are used only for special situations.

The answers to the following questions will help you to understand the importance and usefulness of the drills for you and your team.

—Why use drills?
—How do drills improve team play?
—What are the steps for teaching a drill?
—What are the key principles for effective drills?
—What steps are used to develop a team for match play?

Why use drills? In teaching soccer skills and play patterns, it is not possible to achieve a higher degree of performance without repetition in your practice sessions. During game situations, the frequency of a basic play pattern repetition or the performance of a specific skill does not occur enough to produce economical learning. For this reason, drills performed by small groups of players produce an opportunity for more players to participate more frequently in the action, and simultaneously save time.

Repetition enables you to analyze the players performing in a drill situation more often than you could in a full team situation. Thus, an economical stage is set for correcting the mistakes that the players may make. It is up to you to try correcting undesirable habits and reinforce the desired habitual skills and play patterns.

Drills are for accomplishing an offensive or defensive objective. Even though all players are expected to fill both offensive and defensive assignments, there are special skills and tactics that are unique to the position they play. Yet, ideally, every player should have the skills of a polished striker. Modern soccer requires that the so-called defensive players leave their defensive positions to shoot gaps, overlap, and exchange positions with other players on the team. For this reason, all players should train and practice both offensive and defensive skills and tactics in small groups and through drills designed for the entire team.

The game of soccer is made up of many basic, small encounters;

how the players handle these encounters determines the success of the team. Through the years, certain patterns of play have been recognized as producing the best results, so your job is to help players experience and recognize these patterns and basic plays when they develop on the field. During a game, some of these patterns are repeated while others may occur only once. Through the drilling process, you can set an atmosphere in which these patterns occur more frequently. Through drills, players will reinforce their habitual instinctive response, producing desirable behavior in match play.

How do you use drills to improve team play? At the beginning of each chapter is a section on relating the drills to match play. Understanding these relationships is the first step to success because drills are the foundation of effective match play.

If you see a well-drilled, disciplined team, you see a winner. Match play can be looked at as one long, continuous drill, containing may separate small drills. Drills prepare players to react automatically to a given situation. They help players move a ball without losing possession of it. Drills help a team maneuver the ball into a position that will improve its chance of scoring, and in addition, will help you prepare for an attack at mid-field. Drills also help you set up a defense quickly. Practically every phase of a game can be reproduced and assimilated into drill form. A team that is better prepared to meet the challenges of small-group encounters is more successful in the outcome of match play.

You will notice that many of the drills could be put into chapters other than the one I assigned them to. This is because many of them overlap in function and purpose. For example, this overlapping can be seen in the chapter on shooting, which has a secondary purpose of practicing the skills of passing, receiving and controlling a ball. You should remember that even though these skills are secondary to the purpose, they are important and need as much time and attention as the primary purpose of the drill.

What are the steps for teaching a drill?

1. *Introduce* the drill. Give a brief explanation of how the drill is performed and how it relates to a game situation.
2. *Demonstrate* by using a group of players to walk through the mechanics of the drill.
3. *Explain* the parts of the drill while the demonstration group is performing.
4. *Organize* players into groups; break the players down into the specific number required to perform the drill.
5. *Execute* the drill by having the group carry it out.

6. *Correct* mistakes and reinforce good performances.
7. *Practice* until you are satisfied that learning and understanding have taken place.

What are the key principles for effective drills? There are two types of principles: execution and general. General principles involve background knowledge and understandings relating indirectly to the drilling process. Execution principles relate directly to the process for carrying out the drill.

General principles

—No drill is worth much unless it specifically relates to what happens in a game of soccer.

—Players should be made aware of how the drill relates to the game of soccer.

—Drills should not take up more than a quarter of the practice session, unless a special need for more time is evident. Remember, drilling is only part of a practice session.

—Drills should be introduced at a slow pace and you can gradually increase the performance speed as learning occurs.

—Drills should be modified to accommodate the physical fitness, age and abilities of the players.

—Drills should relate to the system of play that the team is planning to use.

—Drills should be set up to cover all phases of soccer, such as defense, mid-field and attack.

—Drills should be kept simple, and should be easily understood by the players.

—A long-range plan should be developed so that players will receive several types of experiences from a variety of drills.

—Pre-season and early in the season, drills should be used extensively. In mid- and late-season, they can be used as the need develops.

—Drills should move from the simple to the complex. First perform drills without defenders, then against defenders.

—Modify a drill if it doesn't fit your team's needs.

—Drills should not be permitted to become monotonous. A variety of drills will help to keep the interest of the players at a high level.

—As fatigue sets in, technique deteriorates and the quality of learning becomes impaired. Frequent rest periods are recommended to combat this.

—If initial attemps at a drill fail, persistence will pay off.

—Show enthusiasm about the value of drills: it will spread to your players.

—The objective of drilling is to make the players perform automatically when confronted with a similar situation in match play.

Execution principles

—Review the drill procedure before a practice session and make sure you know how it works. Be prepared.

—When introducing a new drill, walk one group of players through it so that the other players can see how it should be performed.

—Avoid talking too much. Get the players into action. Players learn by doing.

—Break the drill down into key steps or key words that will help the players remember the drill sequence. Example: passing order—1 "through," 2 "back," 3 "square."

—Involve as many players as possible in the drill, and don't have players standing around watching. Instead, keep the players active.

—When tactical or technical errors occur, the drill should be interrupted momentarily to correct the error.

—Provide for lanes of traffic that will not interfere with the drill in progress.

—Praise groups that carry the drill out well, and encourage groups having difficulty.

—Caution players about unnecessary roughness, carelessness and dangerous practices.

—If a drill calls for boundary lines, insist that players stay inside them.

—If equipment (flags, cones, etc.) is necessary, have it set up before hand.

—Don't put all the good players in one group. Distribute them evenly so that others can benefit from their example.

—If a defensive and offensive role is required in a drill, make sure players get a chance to experience both.

—Insist on good technique and accuracy.

—Provide a system for ball collecting. Example: after a shot on goal, each player should collect his own ball.

—When a drill calls for a pass on the ground, insist that it be passed on the ground.

—When a drill calls for 1-touch plays or left foot only, insist that players conform.

—In grid drills, the smaller the restricted area, the greater the pressure will be to maintain ball control.

—Encourage players to use feints to conceal their intentions while drilling.

—The final objective of passing drills is efficient ball control.

—Steps in drills are done at a varied pace. Delay is sometimes necessary for certain individuals.

What are the steps used to develop a team for match play? All training systems have good points and bad points. No one training system can solve all of your problems. Your initial starting efforts should be to practice basic skills and work on the physical conditioning of the players.

Next, you may continue training by using the grid system, which is a valuable tool early in the training season, but has its limitations as the season progresses.

Once a team has mastered maneuvers in the squares, it is time to move on to fluid or movement drills. In these drills, players perform maneuvers and patterns while moving down the field.

Next, the practice moves to small-group tactics which include the traditional passing patterns, such as: the wall pass, give and go, scissors, back passes, overlapping screening, decoying, etc. These are traditional passing patterns which have proven to be effective methods of moving the ball.

Finally, practice is directed toward improving both offensive and defensive play by working with a group of players within the team, such as wing and mid-field player, or a goalkeeper and two defenders, etc. Direct practice toward a group of players who work together in a game situation by virtue of the positions they play.

Ultimately, team practice is centered around the scrimmage. During the scrimmage, you interrupt play in order to point out situations and plays that should or should not have transpired. You can also interrupt to introduce special plays and situations which develop during the scrimmage, such as a penalty kick, goal kick or kickoff situation. At this point, the team is practicing small-group tactics in order to emphasize, correct and reinforce a segment of individual and team plays that need attention.

No matter what system or progression you use to prepare your team for match play, the drills in this book will fit into your scheme or plan to accomplish this end. Whether the drills are used in the major development, or merely as a supplementay tool, does not matter.

James P. McGettigan

Acknowledgements

What we know about the game of soccer today comes from a variety of contributions of people genuinely interested in the game. In essence this book is an accumulation of some of their efforts and contributions. Special thanks are extended to those individuals who had the creative insight to develop specific drills, so that preparation for soccer can be done in a more efficient, scientific manner.

My gratitude is extended to all the players I have coached over the years. Their enthusiasm and dedication for soccer was my primary motivation for putting this book together.

Special thanks are extended to Barbara, my wife, for the long hours spent on the diagrams that appear in this book. I would like to extend my gratitude to Joan Milano and Ed Stonehill; to Joan, for her editorial assistance and to Ed, for his graphic assistance and artistic advice.

Contents

Five: Relating Defense and Tackling Drills to Match Play (cont.)

Six: Relating Goalkeeping Drills to Match Play • 100

SECTION TWO: BASIC PATTERNS

Seven: Relating Grid Drills to Match Play • 120

Eight: Relating Moving Passing Drills to Match Play • 127

Eight: Relating Moving Passing Drills to Match Play (cont.)

Running Drill I (lead, square, back) • Drill 8-14: Dutch Passing Running Drill II (lead, square) • Drill 8-15: Dutch Passing Running Drill III (lead passes) • Drill 8-16: Dutch Passing Running Drill IV (lead, square, back) • Drill 8-17: Dutch Passing Running Drill V (lead, square) • Drill 8-18: Pass Through and Overlap • Drill 8-19: Middleman

Nine: Relating Small-Group Passing Drills to Match Play • 145

Drill 9-1: Wall Pass and Shoot • Drill 9-2: Double-Wall Pass • Drill 9-3: Through the Legs • Drill 9-4: Right Mid-Field Cross • Drill 9-5: Mid-Field Setup for a Crisscross • Drill 9-6: Mid-Field Setup for a Straight Run • Drill 9-7: Dribble, Back Pass, and Decoy • Drill 9-8: Long Pass and Decoy • Drill 9-9: Back Pass and Stay • Drill 9-10: Diagonal and Reverse Run • Drill 9-11: Step on it • Drill 9-12: Cross-Decoy • Drill 9-13: Diagonal Decoy and Dribble • Drill 9-14: Opposite Side • Drill 9-15: Back Pass and Go • Drill 9-16: Overlap • Drill 9-17: Two-on-One Commit and Pass Off • Drill 9-18: Scissors • Drill 9-19: Loop Back Decoy • Drill 9-20: Overlap Draw • Drill 9-21: Three on Two Decoy • Drill 9-22: Fake Overlap • Drill 9-23: Fake Draw • Drill 9-24: Heel Drill • Drill 9-25: Switching and Decoy • Drill 9-26: V-Decoy Run • Drill 9-27: Post Man • Drill 9-28: Quick Switching • Drill 9-29: Parallel Leave It • Drill 9-30: Decoy Combination • Drill 9-31: Back Pass Diversion • Drill 9-32: From Behind and Wall Pass • Drill 9-33: Cross Pass and Shoot Cross Pass and Shoot

SECTION THREE: SPECIAL SITUATIONS

Ten: Relating Corner Passing and Corner Kicks to Match Play • 174

Drill 10-1: Two-on-One Wing Cross • Drill 10-2: Straight Wing Cross with a Delayed Run • Drill 10-3: Wing Attack and Recovery • Drill 10-4: Reverse Passing • Drill 10-5: Corner Timing • Drill 10-6: Crisscross Blind Side Run • Drill 10-7: Cross Over Cross • Drill 10-8: Decoy and Cross • Drill 10-9: Overlap and Decoy • Drill 10-10: Wing Crisscross • Drill 10-11: Switching Sides • Drill 10-12: Corner Kick Draw • Drill 10-13: Cross and Shoot • Drill 10-14: Corner Kick Drill I • Drill 10-15: Corner Kick Drill II • Drill 10-16: Corner Kick Drill III • Drill 10-17: Corner Kick Drill IV

Eleven: Relating Throw-In Drills to Match Play • 189

Drill 11-1: Throw-In to the Goalkeeper • Drill 11-2: Tall Man Throw-In • Drill 11-3: Throw-In Pressure • Drill 11-4: Head Return • Drill 11-5: Crisscross Throw-In • Drill 11-6: Give and Go Throw-In with a Decoy •

COMPLETE BOOK
OF DRILLS
FOR WINNING SOCCER

Section One
Skill Drills

Skill is a broad term which encompasses a player's ability to perform a specific task at a certain level of proficiency. It is obvious that skill and technique are prerequisites for developing team tactics and team systems of play. Therefore, the initial efforts in developing a team for match play should be centered around improving each player's skill and technique.

It should be noted, however, that another area of preparation needing attention in the early stages of developing a team is the physical conditioning of the players. Although this can occur concomitantly during practice sessions concentrating on skill development, time should be set aside specifically to improve individuals in this aspect of training. Physical conditioning enables players to perform at a high rate of speed over a prolonged period, specifically 90 minutes. Since proper physical conditioning occurs over a period of time, a portion of every practice session should be devoted to it. You will find more on training and physical conditioning in Section IV.

Skills are learned and perfected in steps. At the beginning, the learner performs skills from a stationary position; then he progresses to a trotting pace, and finally, he performs while running. Another progression is the performance of skills without the resistance of an opponent, then with three-quarters resistance, and finally with all-out pressure from the opponent.

After the initial stages of learning have transpired, the next step is to reinforce this learning by repetition. Repetition is used so that players will be able to perform skills quickly and naturally in a game situation, without having to think about them.

Passing, receiving and controlling are interrelated skills and have therefore been combined. They are included in the first chapter because they are the most important element in the game of soccer, being necessary for effective teamwork and for maintaining possession of the ball.

With the exception of the goalkeeper, all players should practice the skill drills found in Chapters 1 through 5. (Goalkeeper skills drills are found in Chapter 6.) Proficiency in these techniques enables a player to have a broad range of skills to call upon when dealing with individual and group encounters in a game situation.

The following are factors that should be considered when alloting time for skill drills:

1. The time available, the length of the season, and the length of the practice session.
2. The age of the players.
3. The physical condition of the players.
4. The skill level of the players.
5. The ability of the players to learn.
6. The value you place on the drill.

It should be remembered that in the pre-season stage of a training schedule, the greatest amount of time is spent on practicing skills. But as the season progresses, less time is devoted to this endeavor unless a specific need arises.

Through mastery of soccer techniques and skills, individual players can contribute to a team effort with confidence and pride. The skill drills in this section of the book can help you and your team attain these goals.

Chapter One

Relating Passing, Receiving and Controlling Drills to Match Play

Imagine a game of soccer played without passing a ball. Soccer, in its formative stages, found the action of the game centered solely around the ball. Very little conscious passing took place. Everyone bunched in the immediate area of the ball, each trying to shove other players out of the way in order to get a kick at the ball.

As the game developed, the pass was introduced and players were forced to spread out over the field. Further changes were introduced into the game, including rules changes, but the modern game, as we know it today, is a result of the introduction of the pass.

In general, the pass in today's soccer is an instrument of the attacking team. It is the means through which the attacking team is able to develop numerical superiority situations—2 on 1, 3 on 1, etc. It also is the means for taking advantage of these situations after they are developed.

We frequently hear of the controversy about whether the long passing game or the short passing game is best. Rather than looking at this problem in that perspective, we should assess their values as to when, where, and how much these types of passes are used in a game of soccer.

It is a well-known fact that the greatest percentage of passes in a game are short passes. Consequently, I recommend that much of the practice session should be devoted to short passing drills and skills. Granted, a well-timed, long pass is an important weapon in the attack and in the counterattack. Yet, to play a game where the majority of the passes are long is boring, self-defeating, and against sound principles of effective ball control. It has been said that "Most long passes will be kicked back into your face."

Each pass made in a game causes the opponents to move, in order to get into a better position to defend against the new movement of the ball. By moving the ball, two things can happen: First, the opponents move and make the correct adjustment to accommodate the movement, and second, the opponents do not move or move incorrectly. The more the ball moves, the more the opponents must make their adjustments. Thus the chances of an error on the part of the opponents increases.

When these changes take place at a rapid rate, the opponents are likely to make mistakes and, in turn, make incorrect responses to the situation. If these changes take place slowly, the opponents have time to adjust the position of their players to meet the challenges presented by the attackers. In practice passing drills enable players to acquire expertise in moving a ball quickly and frequently. Hopefully, this ability will carry over in the game or to each play situation.

In a game situation, the position of the ball on the field determines the type of movement and, for the most part, the length of the pass. In the defensive third of the field, the ball is moved quickly toward the middle third of the field. Sometimes longer passes are necessary because of the urgency that may develop in this area. The middle third of the field is used for preparing for the attack. This is where the greatest amount of moving the ball occurs, and short passing predominates. As the ball moves into the attacking third of the field, the opponents tighten their defense, and ball movement must become more decisive and direct. Passes in the attack area are long or short, depending upon the opportunities that may develop.

The passing drills found in this section are designed to meet the requirements of each of the three sections of the field—the defense area, midfield, and the attacking section. Many can be used to prepare for use in all three sections of the field. Others are for specific sections of the field.

Passing drills are the first step toward developing team continuity. Through these exercises, players learn to anticipate each other's movements and actions. Players also learn to support one another and to contribute to the unity and cohesion of the team.

The coach who concentrates on drill exercises and creates confidence and expertise among his players in the drill situation will instill confidence in the players in a match play situation.

In relating receiving and controlling drills to match play, it is necessary to understand why these techniques are so important in a modern game of soccer. Quick control is a must. The day when players had all the time they needed to trap the ball, bring it under control and pass it off without too much pressure is gone. Today, tight marking, constant pressure, and the entire team playing defense have speeded up the pace of the game. Instant decisions must be made long before the ball arrives. Players need not only to be able to decide how they are going to bring it under control, but they must also be decisive about what they are going to do with the ball after it is under control.

Quickness in bringing a ball under control helps to insure that players are not rushed in their decisions as to where the ball should be passed in order to further exploit the opponents. In other words, it helps players avoid panic kicking or kicking the ball for the sake of just getting rid of it.

Generally a player can accommodate the approaching angle of a ball, and trap it on the part of the body he intends. If a ball is coming toward him from his right side, he can turn his body so that he is facing the ball. If a ball is decending toward the ground directly in front of him, he can run forward and accommodate it with a thigh or chest trap, rather than waiting for it to fall at his feet. In other words, players can move their bodies to accommodate the angle of the approaching ball. From this we can see the necessity of players, through the drilling process, receiving balls from many directions and from many different heights.

Another variable that must be included in the drilling process to accommodate the reality of match play is the speed of the approaching ball. Players should be drilled to be able to handle balls that are approaching at a fast rate of speed, as well as slow-moving, lofted balls.

Ball control is at its best when the ball is passed on the ground. Then the ball is easier to handle or receive, giving the player passing the ball a direct influence upon how it is received and brought under control. When a player has an opportunity to pass a ball on the ground, but instead carelessly sends it into the air, he robs the receiver some of the time he could have used to prepare for his next pass or encounter. In other words, the passer can add pressure onto the player receiving the ball.

In receiving and controlling drills, the receiver should be encouraged to run and meet the ball, rather than standing and waiting for it. The few steps he may take toward the oncoming ball could give him time to make a decision as to what his next move will be.

The skills involved in controlling and receiving a ball in match play, such as collecting, turning and moving the ball, are performed as a unit or as one skill. Yet beginners need to practice each skill separately, and as they develop, should be encouraged to practice these skills as a unit. The purpose of combining these skills into a single unit is that it enables a player to be able to gain the extra time needed to make his next decision in a game situation.

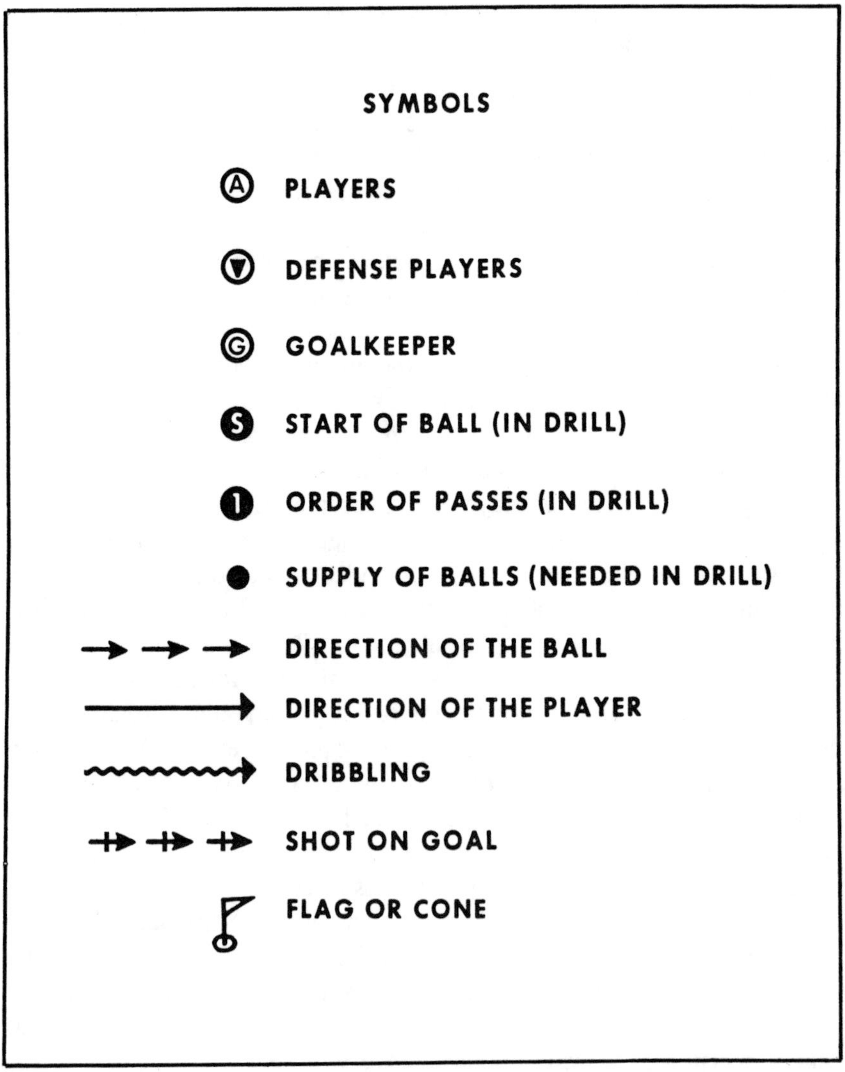

SYMBOLS

Ⓐ **PLAYERS**

▼ **DEFENSE PLAYERS**

Ⓖ **GOALKEEPER**

Ⓢ **START OF BALL (IN DRILL)**

❶ **ORDER OF PASSES (IN DRILL)**

● **SUPPLY OF BALLS (NEEDED IN DRILL)**

→ → → **DIRECTION OF THE BALL**

———→ **DIRECTION OF THE PLAYER**

∿∿∿→ **DRIBBLING**

⊶⊶⊶ **SHOT ON GOAL**

⚑ **FLAG OR CONE**

Drill 1–1   Ball Turn and Pass

No. of players   3 per drill group

Equipment   2 soccer balls—B has a ball and C has a ball.

Distance   A to B—10 to 12 yards, A to C—10 to 12 yards.

Explanation   Player A passes to player B. B returns the pass to A. Then
B turns 180 degrees and receives a pass from C, and in the same manner
B returns the pass to C and turns 180 degrees, etc. This drill is continued
for one minute, then players change positions. It is important that the
players keep pressure on player B. As soon as player B starts to turn, he
should receive a pass. Insist on "crisp" (fast and snappy) passes on the
ground passes.

Purpose   The primary purpose is to improve individuals' muscular endurance. The secondary purpose is to improve passing, receiving, and
controlling the ball.

Variation   Use one ball per drill group. In this variation, A and C turn
360 degrees with the ball and pass back to player B. B passes to A. A
turns 360 degrees with the ball, and passes back to B. B turns 180 degrees
and passes to C, and the drill continues.

Variation   Use 2 balls per drill group. In this variation, A passes to B
and B passes back to A. Then C throws his ball at B, and B heads back
to C.

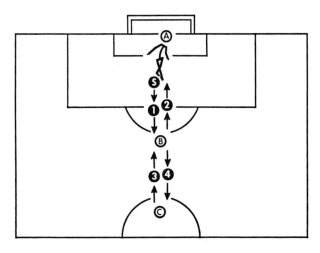

Drill 1–1

Ball Turn and Pass

Drill 1–2   4-Man Return Pass

No. of players   4 per drill group.

Distance   B to C—2 yards, A to B—4 to 6 yards, C to D—4 to 6 yards.

Equipment   2 balls per group.

Explanation   B faces A and C faces D. On a signal, A passes to B. B passes back to A. At the same time, D passes to C. C passes back to D. B and C exchange positions. A passes to C while D passes to B, and so on. Repeat.

Purpose   This is a pressure passing drill, used to improve muscular endurance. Players practice trapping a ball, and the middle 2 players practice passing and exchanging positions.

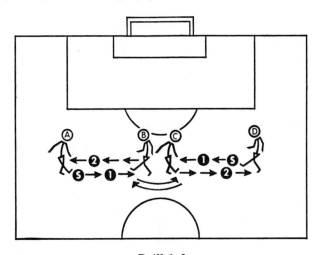

Drill 1–2

4-Man Return Pass

Drill 1–3   "1-Touch" Overlap

No. of players   3 per drill group

Distance   A to C—10 to 12 yards.

Explanation   Player A passes to player C and runs behind player C. Player C passes to player B and runs behind player B. Player B passes to A and runs behind player A. Repeat this cycle. All passes should be "1-touch" passes.

Purpose   This drill is designed to practice "1-touch" passing. Once players become accustomed to this drill, it can be used to improve muscular endurance.

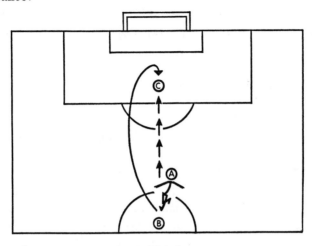

Drill 1–3

"1-Touch" Overlap

Drill 1–4   2-Man Outside the Flag Passing

No. of players   2 per drill group.

Equipment   2 cones or flags.

Distance   Flags are 10 to 15 yards apart. A to B—10 to 12 yards.

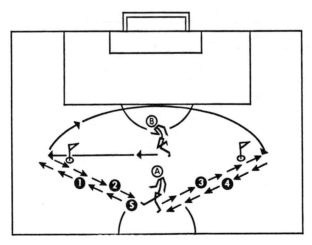

Drill 1–4

2-Man Outside the Flag Passing

Explanation A passes to B outside of the flags. B returns the pass outside of the flags. B then runs to the area outside of the other flag. A then passes to the other side (outside the flags), and B returns the pass.

Purpose Players practice passing and receiving the ball. Players improve their muscular endurance.

Drill 1–5 Figure-8 Return Pass

No. of players 3 per drill group.

Distance Flags—10 to 12 yards apart. A to the flags—5 yards.

Equipment 2 flags or cones, 2 soccer balls.

Explanation C runs around the cone or flag and receives a pass from A. C returns the pass to A and immediately runs around the other cone or flag and receives a pass from B. C returns the pass to A and immediately runs around the other cone or flag and receives a pass from B. C returns the pass to B and repeats the cycle.

Purpose Players practice receiving and passing the ball. Players also improve their muscular endurance.

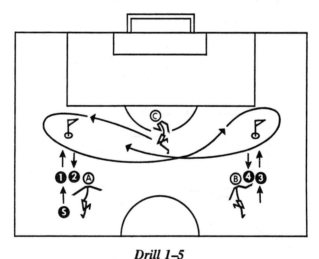

Drill 1–5

Figure-8 Return Pass

Drill 1–6 Figure-8 Flag Passing

No. of players 3 per drill group.

Distance   Flags—10 to 15 yards apart, A and B to the flags—5 to 7 yards.

Equipment   2 cones or flags, 2 soccer balls.

Explanation   C runs around the flag and receives a pass from A. C returns the pass to A and continues around the other flag to receive a pass from B. C returns the pass to B and so on. Before each pass, player C dribbles the ball a short distance before passing back.

Purpose   Players practice receiving, passing, and dribbling a ball. Player C improves his muscular endurance.

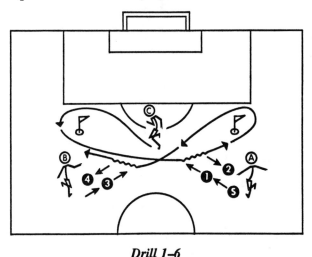

Drill 1–6

Figure-8 Flag Passing

Drill 1–7   Middleman Pressure

No. of players   5 per drill group.

Distance   E to the other players—5 to 10 yards.

Explanation   Each man, in his turn, passes to the middle player starting with player A. A passes to E, and E passes back to A. Repeat the same to B, C, and D. E should be kept under pressure. As soon as E passes back, the next ball should be on its way. Passes should be crisp and on the ground.

Purpose   Players practice quick control and quick return passing. Players improve their muscular endurance.

Variation   Use 4 players. The 3 outside players form a triangle; the 4th player is in the middle of the triangle.

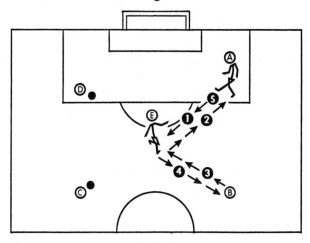

Drill 1–7

Middleman Pressure

Drill 1–8   5-Man Overlap

No. of players   5 per drill group.

Distance   Players form a 10 to 15 yard square.

Explanation   A passes to B. A overlaps and takes B's place. B passes to

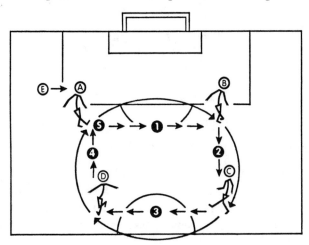

Drill 1–8

5-Man Overlap

C and overlaps and takes C's place, etc. As soon as A passes to B, E steps into the square and takes the place that player A vacated.

Purpose This drill teaches players to overlap and to fill in the space provided by the player who previously vacated the space. The primary purpose of this drill is to build muscular endurance. The number of repetitions depends upon the physical condition of the players.

Drill 1–9 Square Overlap

No. of players   12 to 20 per drill group.

Distance   A to B—15 to 20 yards, A to D—15 to 20 yards.

Explanation   A passes to player B. A gets in the end of B's line. B passes to C, and B gets in the back of C's line, etc. 2 balls are used to increase the pace of this drill. One ball is started at line A, and the other ball is started at line C.

Purpose   Players practice passing, trapping, and overlapping. This drill can be used as a warm-up drill or activity.

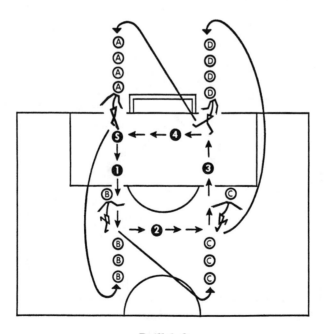

Drill 1–9

Square Overlap

Drill 1–10   Continuous Passing Drill

No. of players   12 to 20 per drill group.

Distance   A to D—20 yards, A to C—10 yards.

Explanation   Positions A and C pass the ball diagonally across the rect-angle. Players B and D pass the ball straight ahead. After a player passes the ball, he gets in back of the line that received his pass. While criss-crossing, players should be careful not to impede the progress of the other players.

Purpose   Players practice passing and receiving the ball on the ground. This drill can be used as a pre-game warm-up.

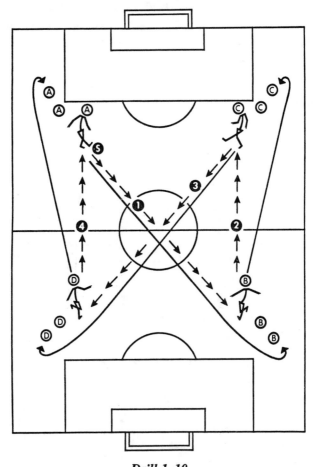

Drill 1–10

Continuous Passing Drill

Variation   Use two balls and start the second ball at the same point where the first ball was started. Players can learn to use 4 balls in performing this drill.

Drill 1–11   Musical Flags

No. of players   5 per drill group.

Distance   A to B—15 yards, B to D—5 to 10 yards.

Equipment   6 cones or 6 flags.

Explanation   A passes to B and sprints to occupy the flag or cone that does not have a man standing beside it. B passes to C and sprints to the unoccupied flag, and so on.

Purpose   Players learn to fill in the space that has been vacated. This is an excellent drill to practice "1-touch" passing. This drill is used to improve players' physical fitness.

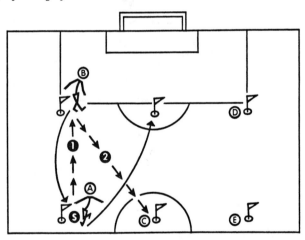

Drill 1–11

Musical Flags

Drill 1–12   6 Man "1-Touch" Give and Go

No. of players   6 per drill group.

Distance   A to B—10 to 12 yards.

Explanation   Line A and line B face each other, as shown on the diagram. Play starts when player A passes diagonally to his left to the open space, to player B. Then A runs diagonally to his right. B runs and meets the ball. B immediately passes (square) back to A. A passes to B's line. A gets in the back of B's line, and B gets in back of A's line. This procedure is repeated by player B passing to his left, etc. A player passes diagonally to his left, and runs diagonally to his right.

Purpose   The primary purpose of this drill is for players to practice "give-and-go" passes. Players practice passing and running to the open space. The secondary purpose is to improve players' physical condition.

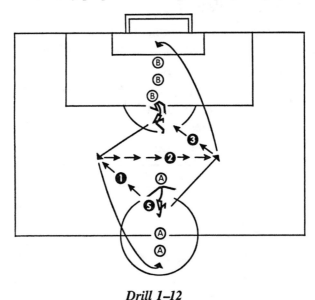

Drill 1–12

6 Man "1-Touch" Give and Go

Drill 1–13   6 Man Continuous Pass

No. of players   8 to 10 per drill group.

Distance   A to B—5 to 7 yards, C to D—5 to 7 yards, B to C—2 to 3 yards.

Equipment   2 soccer balls.

Explanation   Players A and D each have a ball. Players A and D pass to the center players. A to B and D to C. After passing, players A and D run diagonally to receive a diagonal pass back from players B and C, respectively. The balls are returned to the first players in the opposite lines, and the play is started again.

Purpose This drill is used as a warm-up. It is also practice for the basic "give-and-go" play. Players practice passing and moving to the open space.

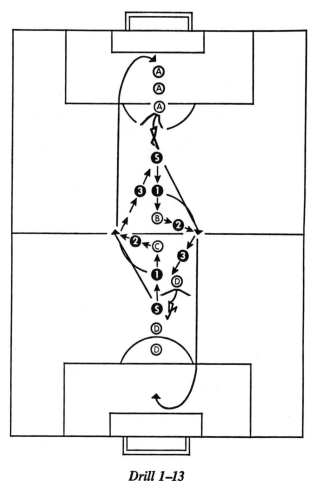

Drill 1–13

6 Man Continuous Pass

Drill 1–14   2-Man Curving Drill

No. of players   2 per drill group.

Distance   A to the corner of the 18 yard line—5 to 10 yards.

Equipment   1 ball per player.

Explanation   Player A attempts to curve the ball around behind the goal to player B. Players change lines.

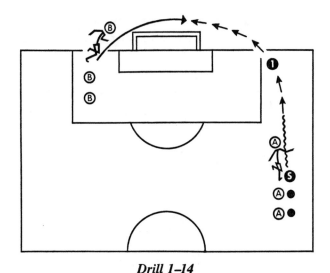

Drill 1–14

2-Man Curving Drill

Purpose   Player A practices curving a ball around the goal post. Sometimes in a game situation it is necessary to swerve a ball around a defender when the defender blocks the direct pathway of a pass.

Variation   Flags can be placed in the field, so players can practice curving the ball around the flags.

Drill 1–15   Quick Switching

No. of players   12 or more.

Distance   G to A and B—15 yards, A to B—15 yards to 20 yards.

Equipment   4 flags or cones or 2 small goals, 10 or more soccer balls.

Explanation   G rolls the first ball out to player A. A crosses the ball to C, who is cutting down the field toward the goal. C shoots at the goal. G rolls the second ball to player B. B crosses the ball to D, who is cutting down the field toward the goal. D shoots at the goal. Players in lines C and D change lines after each shot at the goal. C and D, after each shot at the goal, retrieve their own balls and carry them back to the goalkeeper—G. In this way, a constant flow of balls is available.

Purpose   Players practice the following: quick changes from defense to offense; switching the ball to the other side of the field; and chipping, trapping, dribbling, and shooting. Goalkeepers practice beginning or starting an attack.

Drill 1–15

Quick Switching

Drill 1-16   Mid-Field Look Up

No. of players   6 per drill group.

Distance   D, E, F, G, and H to A—5 to 10 yards apart.

Equipment   A supply of soccer balls.

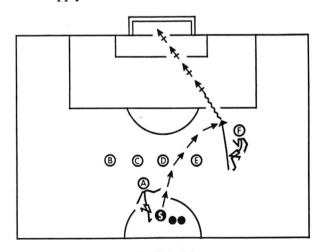

Drill 1–16

Mid-Field Look Up

Explanation   The coach yells out a letter, such as ''F.'' This is a signal for player F to run toward the goal. Player A must look up and chip the ball to the player breaking toward the goal. Player A should be mid-field.

Purpose   Players practice chipping, trapping, dribbling, and shooting. This is a good drill to get mid-field players to look up before passing the ball.

Variation   Use additional players to work with player A. These 2 players pass a ball back and forth until a letter is called. When a letter is called, these players get the pass off quickly to the player moving toward the goal.

Drill 1–17   Penalty Area Pressure Passing

No. of players   5 per drill group.

Equipment   1 flag or cone and 4 soccer balls.

Explanation   Players A, C, D, and E take up the position seen on the diagram, with each player on the corner of the 18-yard line with a ball on the ground in front of him. Play starts with player B receiving a pass from player A. B passes back to A. B then runs around the flag and receives a pass from C. B passes back to C, and once again runs around the flag and receives a pass from player D, and so on. B repeats the entire cycle 2 times.

Purpose   Players learn to receive and return a pass from many direc-

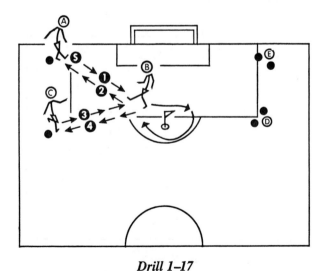

Drill 1–17

Penalty Area Pressure Passing

tions. This drill is used to improve speed and muscular endurance, while at the same time, giving practice in passing and receiving a ball. The intensity with which this drill is executed depends upon the speed at which A, C, D, and E pass the ball to player B. The secondary purpose of this drill is to improve "1-touch" passing.

Drill 1–18   Long-Pass Drill

No. of players   3 per drill group.

Distance   A to B—35 to 45 yards, B to C—35 to 40 yards.

Explanation   A makes a long pass to B. B passes across the field to the 18-yard restraining arc to player C. C shoots at the goal.

Purpose   Players practice passing long distances.

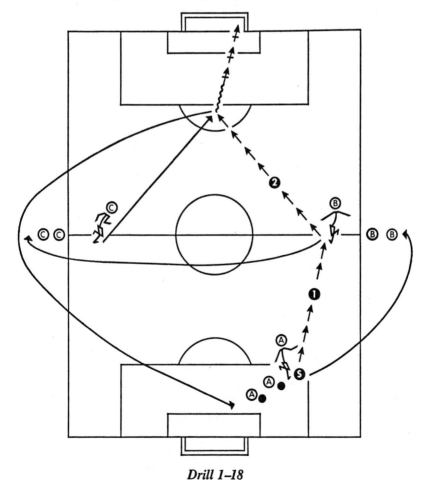

Drill 1–18

Long-Pass Drill

Drill 1–19   Chipping Over the Middleman

No. of players   3 per drill group.

Distance   A to B—20 to 30 yards.

Explanation   A chips the ball over the defensive player to player B. A and the defensive player move forward, and B chips over the defensive player, and so on. The defensive player must stay midway between players A and B.

Purpose   The primary purpose of this drill is to practice chipping a ball over a defender's head.

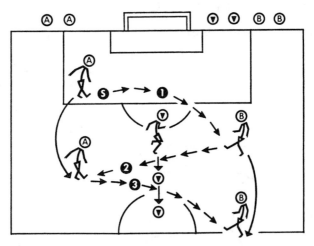

Drill 1–19

Chipping Over the Middleman

Drill 1–20   Restricted Zone

No. of players   2 per drill group.

Equipment   10 flags or cones, 1 soccer ball per every 2 players.

Explanation   From end line to end line, the field is divided into 3 sections: the restricted section in the middle and the 2 outside sections, called the passing and receiving sections. From touchline to touchline, the field is further divided into 4 zones. Both players, A and B, must successfully pass a ball over the restricted sections before moving to the next zone. There are 2 requirements in performing this drill: (1) the ball must be kicked from one passing zone to the other without its touching the ground in the restricted section; (2) the ball must be trapped and controlled before it goes out of bounds. This second stipulation promotes accuracy. Players must meet these two requirements before moving to the next zone. Both A and B are required to perform both phases of this drill, kicking and receiving, before they move to the next zone to repeat the same procedure.

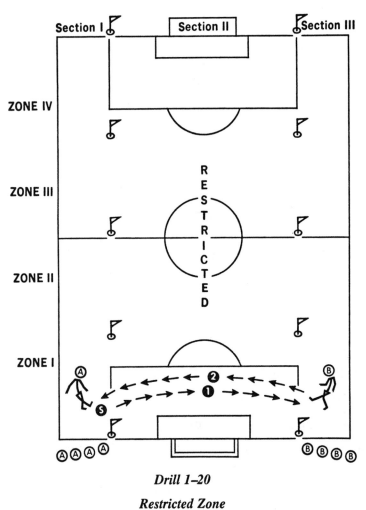

Drill 1–20

Restricted Zone

Drill 1–21   Center Circle Control

No. of players   3 per drill group.

Distance   B to defensive players—1 to 2 yards, B to A—10 to 15 yards.

Explanation   A throws a ball in the center circle and yells "Go!" B and the defensive player race to see who can get control of the ball. When B is able to get control of the ball, he must stay in the circle for 5 seconds. The defensive player tries to clear the ball out of the circle, and starts 1 or 2 steps behind player B, in order to give player B a slight advantage.

Purpose   Player B practices quick control of the ball under the pressure and presence of a defensive player.

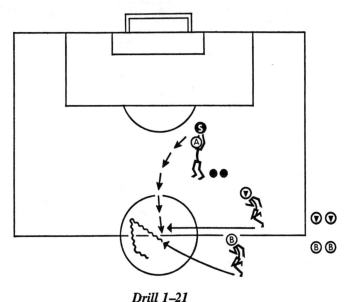

Drill 1–21

Center Circle Control

Drill 1–22   "1-Touch" 6-Man Passing

No. of players   6 per drill group.

Distance   A to B—10 to 15 yards.

Explanation   A passes to B, then gets in back of B's line. B passes to A, then gets in back of A's line.

Purpose   Players practice "1-touch" push passes. This drill can be used as a warm-up activity.

Drill 1–23   Continuous Wall Pass

No. of players   6 or more.

Distance   A to C—20 to 30 yards, C to D—30 to 40 yards, D to E—20 to 30 yards, E to B—30 to 40 yards.

Explanation   C, D, and E are stationary players. A throws, and starts the drill. B runs past A and receives a pass from A. B dribbles toward C. C

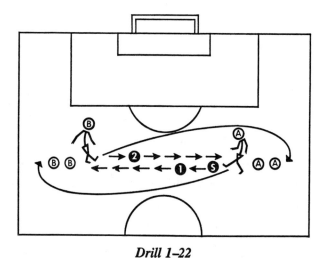

Drill 1–22

"1-Touch" 6-Man Passing

yells "pass," and B passes to C. C passes back to B and B continues, repeating the same procedure with D and E. B finally puts his ball near A, and gets into the back of the line with the B players.

Purpose Players improve their physical conditioning. Players practice continuous wall passes.

Drill 1–23

Continuous Wall Pass

Drill 1–24 Circle Passing on the Move

No. of players 10 to 20.

Distance   A to B—10 to 15 yards.

Equipment   1 ball per A team.

Explanation   A players dribble their ball in a counter-clockwise circle. When the opportunity arises, they attempt to pass their ball past B players and into the center of the circle. All players must pass on the ground. When B players get possession of the ball, they must kick it back to the A players who attempt the kick. Play is continuous.

Purpose   A players practice feinting and passing through gaps made by the players. B players practice quick control and other trapping skills.

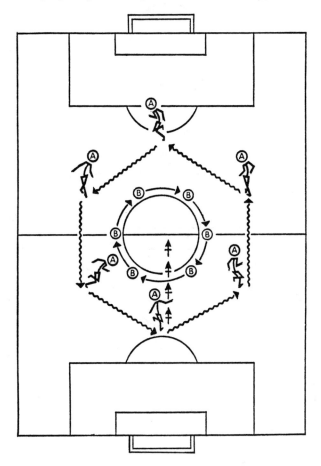

Drill 1–24

Circle Passing on the Move

Drill 1–25 Meet the Pass (No Diagram)

No. of players 2 per drill group.

Distance A and B are 30 to 40 yards apart, facing each other.

Explanation A kicks the ball to player B. B sprints forward to meet the ball. B traps it, turns it, and dribbles back to the original place where he started. Repeat the same drill with B kicking to player A. The ball can be kicked on the ground or in the air.

Purpose Players practice running to meet the ball, and receiving and controlling the ball.

Drill 1–26 Volley Drill (No Diagram)

No. of players 2 per drill group.

Distance A to B—10 to 15 yards apart. A and B are facing each other.

Equipment 1 ball per 2 players, goalpost and crossbar.

Explanation A throws a ball over the goalpost toward player B. Player B volley kicks the ball back over the goalpost to player A.

Drill 1–27 Catching the Ball (No Diagram)

No. of players 2 per drill group.

Distance A to B—10 to 15 yards apart.

Equipment 1 ball per 2 players.

Explanation A and B are facing each other. Player A throws the ball in the air toward and near player B. B tries to catch the ball on his instep, and tries to place it on the ground. Emphasize that the ball should stick to the instep before it is placed on the ground.

Purpose Players practice trapping the ball.

Drill 1–28 Circle Passing (No Diagram)

No. of players 5 per drill group, 3 on the outside of the circle and 2 defenders on the inside of the center circle.

Explanation Players A, B, and C pass the ball around the center circle line (10 yard radius). Each pass must touch some part of the center circle line. Two defensive players attempt to intercept and get control of the ball. Defensive players cannot leave the center circle. A, B, and C are permitted to move around the outside of the circle to support each other.

Purpose   Players practice passing, trapping, and supporting each other around a restricted area.

Drill 1–29   Overhead Kicking and Back Heading (No Diagram)

No. of players   3 per drill group.

Distance   A and B face each other—10 to 12 yards apart; A to C, with A's back to C—10 to 12 yards apart.

Explanation   B loops the ball to A. A kicks or heads the ball back over his head to player C without turning around. A then turns and faces C and repeats the same procedure.

Purpose   Players practice over-the-head kicking and/or backward heading.

Chapter Two

Relating Heading Drills to Match Play

In a game of soccer, the technique of heading is used to pass a ball, control a ball, deflect a ball, shoot a ball, and defensively, clear a ball.

Many can play the game of soccer adequately with their feet, but fall short when the skill of heading a ball comes into play. Without heading ability, a player will miss many opportunities to get control of the ball, make a quick, safe pass out of a congested area, score goals or create scoring opportunities for himself and his teammates. Expertise in heading skills is like "the icing on the cake." Fearless, effective headers can be the difference between losing or winning a game.

Today's game, being highly defensive because of the four-back defensive system and the defensive-sweeper system, makes heading ability a valuable tool for an individual and a team when attacking another team. Modern defensive systems make it difficult to work the ball on the ground and through the defense. Consequently, attackers must go to the air and over the defense. Conversely, you can see a strong need for the defensive players to be able to head the ball in order to clear it out of the immediate area surrounding the goal, preventing a score.

Frequently, a player finds himself unable to bring a ball to his feet because of the close marking of an opponent. In this case, he must head into an open space and chase the ball to maintain possession, or he may decide to head the ball into an open space to another teammate. Seasoned players know the value of controlling and moving the ball on the ground. Passing on the ground is the safest way to move the ball and still maintain possession of it. Yet, when the ball does leave the ground, you should use the quickest technique possible to bring it back to the ground where it can be controlled and moved safely. In this instance, the head can be a valuable tool.

On a throw-in, it is a common practice for the player receiving the throw-in to head it back to the thrower since the thrower is rarely marked by an opposing player.

During a game, a player is called upon to head a ball in practically every direction—forward, over the head, to himself, at the goal, sidewards, diving, etc. For this reason, I have provided a variety of heading practice drills.

You can find other heading drills in Chapter 1 on passing and in Chapter 4 on shooting. Since heading at the goal can be considered a shot on goal, and a head to a teammate can be considered a pass, some of the heading drills were included in other sections of this book. Further heading drills can be found in Chapter 11, on throw-ins.

Drill 2–1   3 Variations of Heading Drills

No. of players   2 per drill group.

Distance   A to B—10 to 15 yards.

Explanation   A throws the ball high to player B. B heads the ball back to A.

Purpose   Players practice head trapping and other heading skills.

Variation   A throws the ball high to player B. B bounces the ball on his head once then heads it back to A (2-touch heading).

Variation   A throws to B, and B heads back to A as they move down the field facing each other.

Variation   A throws to B, and B heads back to A as A runs forward down the field, while B runs backward. The same drill can be performed with A running backward and B running forward.

Note   In all the moving variations, the players reverse roles. In other words, A becomes the header and B becomes the thrower.

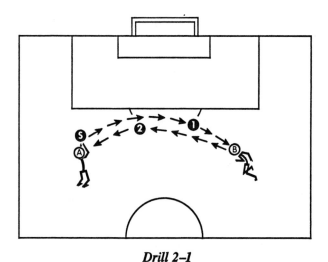

Drill 2–1

3 Variations of Head Drills

Drill 2–2   Heading Pressure

No. of players   4 per drill group.

Distance   A to B—5 yards, B to the defensive player—1 yard, C to A—5 yards.

Equipment   A supply of balls.

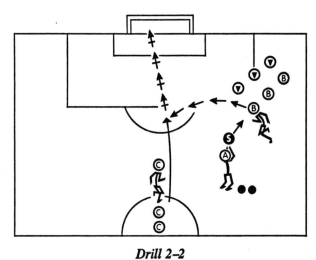

Drill 2–2

Heading Pressure

Explanation   A throws the ball high in the air to player B. B heads to the space in front of player C. C collects the ball and takes a shot at the goal. The defensive player attempts to harass player B by making it difficult for B to head the ball to player C. The defensive player provides three-quarters resistance.

Purpose   Players practice heading while being pressured by a defensive player.

Drill 2–3   Side Heading

No. of players   3 per drill group.

Distance   A to B—44 yards.

Explanation   A chips a ball high across and in front of the goal. B heads the ball down and into the goal. The goalkeeper must stay on the goal line.

Purpose   Players practice heading at the goal, while approaching the goal from the side. Player A practices chipping the ball.

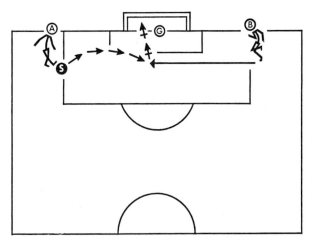

Drill 2–3

Side Heading

Drill 2–4   Head Shooting

No. of players   2 per drill group.

Distance   A to B—20 to 30 yards.

Explanation   A throws the ball (head high) to player B as B runs toward the goal. Players are encouraged to head the ball down and to put force into their heading.

Purpose   Players practice heading skills.

Variation   The ball is thrown close to the ground, forcing A to dive, in order to head the ball.

Caution   When dive-heading, players should be instructed in the proper technique of landing on the ground to prevent injuries.

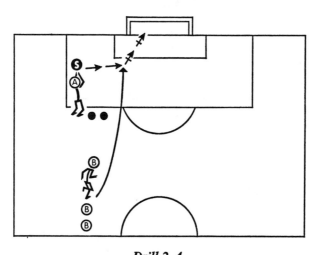

Drill 2–4

Head Shooting

Drill 2–5   Pressure Heading

No. of players   4 per drill group.

Distance   A to B—20 yards, B to C—20 yards, B to the flags—5 to 10 yards.

Equipment   1 flag or cone, 3 soccer balls.

Explanation   A, B, and C stand outside the 18-yard area with a ball in their hands. D runs toward A. A throws the ball into the air toward D. D heads back to A. D then runs around the cone and toward B, and so on. Repeat this drill 3 times or more, depending upon the condition of the players.

Purpose   Players improve speed and muscular endurance. Players practice heading skills.

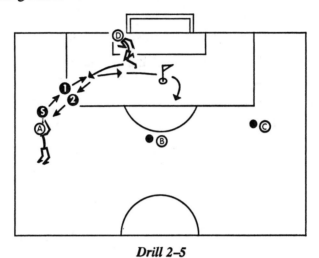

Drill 2–5

Pressure Heading

Drill 2–6   2-Man Heading Drill

No. of players   2 per drill group.

Distance   A to B—15 to 20 yards, B to the Flags—20 yards. Flags are 20 to 30 yards apart.

Explanation   B runs around one of the flags and heads a ball thrown high by player A. B heads it back to A. B immediately runs around to the other flag and repeats the same procedure.

Purpose   Players improve their muscular endurance and their heading technique.

Drill 2–7   2-Man Heading Exercises (No Diagram)

No. of players   2 per drill group.

Distance   A to B—1 to 2 yards apart.

Explanation   A throws the ball to B, and B heads the ball back to A. B is in a sitting position.

Variation   A throws the ball to B, and B heads the ball back to A. B is in a kneeling position.

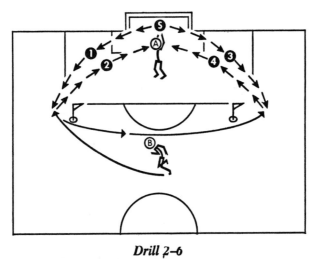

Drill 2-6

2 Man Heading Drill

Variation   A throws the ball to B, and B heads back to A. A is in a push-up position. B moves forward to head the ball.

Variation   A holds the ball at arm's length over his head and B tries to head the ball out of A's hands. A faces away from B.

Variation   A throws a ball to B. B executes a sit-up and heads the ball back to A. A should time his throw so that the ball arrives as B completes his sit-up.

Purpose   Players practice heading skills from various body positions.

Chapter Three

Relating Dribbling, Feinting and Screening Drills to Match Play

Dribbling is a technique used by players to push a ball along the ground with the inside, the outside and the sole of the foot. When the opponents are in the immediate area of the dribbler, it is crucial that the dribbler is able to make instant contact with the ball in order to maintain possession of the ball. If the ball gets too far away from the dribbler, an opponent is likely to steal it and win possession of the ball. When an opponent is not in the immediate area of the dribbler, or when a breakaway is eminent near a goal, dribblers sometimes push the ball farther in front of themselves. They do this to increase their speed to take advantage of the situation.

In match play, dribbling the ball can be justified in various situations. Yet players should observe the general rule that a player should not dribble if he can make a safe pass. Since we know that passing opportunities are not always available, the only thing left to do with the ball is to dribble it until you get an opportunity to pass it off.

The following are situations when dribbling might be justified:

1. When an attacking player finds himself in a situation where he is faced with only one defender between him and the goal.
2. When dribbling is used to lure defenders out of position to create open space for a pass.
3. When dribbling is used until a safe pass is available.
4. When the defenders are not applying pressure and a safe pass is not available.
5. When an attacker has beaten the last defender and he wants to get closer to the goal for a shot at the goal.

Feinting and screening techniques are used in match play to protect a ball till the time comes when it can be safely passed or shot at the goal. Further, these techniques are used to deceive your opponents. You make your opponents think you are going in one direction and you quickly go in another direction. In a change of pace maneuver, you slow down to make your opponent slow down, then you sprint off. Thus, you lull your opponent into thinking you will continue to run slowly. When he slows down to accommodate your pace, sprint off leaving him behind.

Defenders use feinting techniques to unnerve attackers by pretending to rush in for a tackle, only backing off at the last moment. Hopefully, this will cause an attacker to make a mistake. Further, a defender uses a simple shoulder swerve to force an attacker to change his route and go in the direction that he, the defender, wants.

Screening is a technique in which a player maintains possession of a ball by shielding it from an opponent's vision. You place your body between the ball and the opponent. This procedure is necessary in order to gain time for a teammate to get free and become available for a pass.

Most of the emphasis in this chapter is dribbling, but feinting and screening techniques should be combined with dribbling drills. For example, in the slalom dribbling drill, players should perform feinting and screening maneuvers before they dribble around the flag. These skills must be learned in a combined state to be effective later in match play. Therefore you need to provide drills to give frequent and varied experiences in dribbling, feinting and screening a ball. You should expose players to a variety of experiences in these areas.

Preparation in regard to dribbling, feinting and screening techniques is, for the most part, an individual matter. Through game experience, players learn what works for them.

Drill 3–1   Dribble and Outside-the-Foot Pass

No. of players   6 per drill group.

Distance   A to B—20 to 30 yards.

Explanation   A dribbles until he is alongside of B. At this point, A square passes to B, and goes to the back of B's line. B then repeats the same procedure.

Purpose   Players practice dribbling and outside-of-the-foot passing.

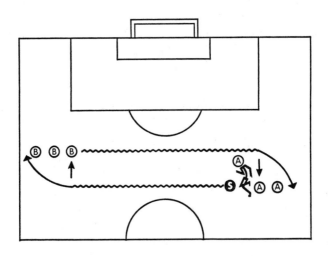

Drill 3–1

Dribble and Outside the Foot Pass

Drill 3–2   Slalom Dribble (No Diagram)

No. of players   10 or more.

Distance   The cones or flags are 2 or 3 yards apart.

Equipment   10 or more cones or flags.

Explanation   Players dribble in and out of the flags or cones. When they reach the last flag, they turn back and dribble against the traffic. This drill requires concentration on the part of the players.

Variation   All players dribble backward by pulling the ball through and around the cones, using the sole of the foot.

Variation   Players dribble 360 degrees around each cone or flag.

Variation   If using cones, players jump over each cone.

Purpose   Players improve dribbling and feinting skills. Players become accustomed to the feel of the ball.

Drill 3–3   Dribbling and Feinting

No. of players   2 per drill group.

Distance   Flags—2 rows with 2 yards between flags. 10 yards between rows. A to B—5 to 10 yards.

Explanation   On a signal (whistle), the first player in each line dribbles and feints his way through the flags and shoots at the goal. The shot at the goal should be taken on the outside of the last flag.

Purpose   Players practice dribbling, feinting, and shooting.

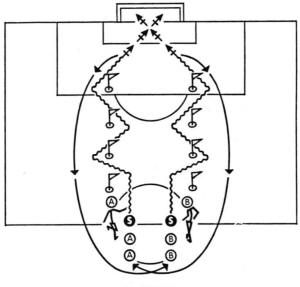

Drill 3–3

Dribbling and Feinting

Drill 3–4   Stop and Go Random Dribble (No Diagram)

No. of players   The number of players depends upon the size of the confined area. Players should have enough space to permit movement, yet the area for dribbling should be congested. The penalty area is frequently used for this drill. In the penalty area, use 20 or more players.

Explanation Each player dribbles his ball inside a confined area. When the coach blows the whistle, all players stand still and stop their ball by placing the sole of their foot on top of the ball. On the second whistle, dribbling is resumed.

Purpose Players practice dribbling and feinting skills in a conjested area.

Variation When the whistle is blown, the players change direction.

Variation Place defensive players among the dribblers. The defensive players attempt to clear balls out of the confined area.

Drill 3–5   One Bounce Down the Field (No Diagram)

No. of players 1.

Equipment 1 soccer ball per player.

Explanation A player moves his ball down the field by kicking his ball forward, approximately 10 feet into the air. When the ball hits the ground, the player kicks forward again before the ball hits the ground a second time.

Variation Player kicks the ball before it hits the ground.

Purpose Players practice juggling skills while moving down the field, and improve their ball-handling skills.

Drill 3–6   Cross the Defensive Zone

No. of players 3 per drill group.

Distance and equipment 4 cones or flags to mark off a 5-yard wide by 25-yard long defense zone.

Explanation Player A attempts to pass a ball through the defense zone while a defense player slides back and forth to obstruct the path of the ball. At the same time, attempts are made to pass the ball through this zone. Players dribble and feint in order to create a clear pathway for a through pass to the player on the other side of the grid.

Purpose Players practice feinting and dribbling. Players also practice getting free in order to receive a pass. This is known as running off the ball.

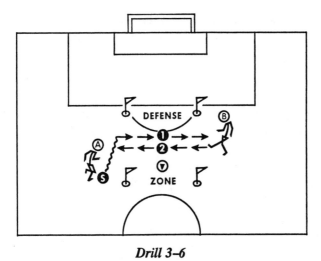

Drill 3–6

Cross the Defensive Zone

Drill 3–7 One-on-One Tease (No Diagram)

No. of players 2 per drill group.

Distance At the start of the drill—A to the defensive player—3 yds.

Explanation With his foot on top of a ball before him, A faces the defensive player. A does not move until the defensive player attempts to reach for the ball with his foot. At this time, A attempts to dribble around the defensive player and over the finish line.

Variation A begins the drill with his back to the defensive player. When the defensive player attempts to get around to the front of player A, A turns away from the defensive player and dribbles over the finish line.

Purpose Players practice dribbling and feinting skills. Defensive players learn not to reach for the ball unless they are 100% sure of gaining possession of the ball.

Drill 3–8 Down the Middle

No. of players 2 per drill group.

Distance 4 flags placed on the corners of the 20-yard square in front of the goal area.

Explanation   A dribbles between the flags and tries to beat the defensive player. A must stay within the confines of the flags while dribbling toward the goal. A must get past the last set of flags before he can shoot at the goal. To increase the pressure on player A, decrease the size of the square.

Purpose   Players practice dribbling and feinting skills in a confined area. Defense players practice tackling and clearing skills.

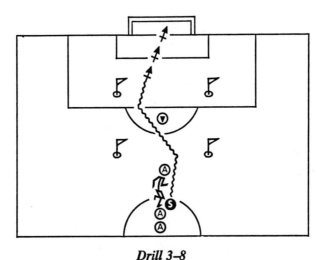

Drill 3–8

Down the Middle

Drill 3–9   Push-Pull Alternate-Drag (No Diagram)

No. of players   1.

Equipment   1 soccer ball per player.

Explanation   Each player moves his ball down the field in the following ways:

1. By pushing the ball with the sole of the left foot 4 times.
2. By pushing the ball with the sole of the right foot 4 times.
3. By pushing alternately with the sole of the right foot and with the sole of the left foot.
4. By pulling the ball 4 times with the sole of the right foot while moving backwards.

5. By repetition of step 4 using the left foot.
6. By alternately pulling the ball 4 times with your left foot while moving backwards.
7. By dragging the ball 4 times with your right foot while facing the sidelines.
8. By repeating step 7 using the left foot.

Purpose Players practice dribbling and feinting skills. Players become accustomed to the feel of the ball. This drill is used in the early phase of a training season.

Drill 3–10 Speed Dribble

No. of players 2 per drill group.

Distance A to B—20 to 25 yards, A to C—20 to 25 yards.

Explanation On a signal (whistle), players A, B, and C dribble toward the goal. The defensive players attempt to get ahead of A, B, and C to clear the ball. Long kicking is not permitted by the dribblers. A, B, and C are not allowed to shoot the ball until they pass over the penalty area line.

Purpose Players A, B, and C practice speed-dribbling under pressure. The defensive players practice recovery maneuvers and clearing the ball.

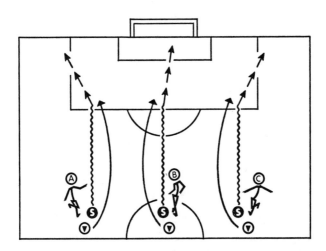

Drill 3–10

Speed Dribble

Drill 3–11   Flag—Head, Trap, Dribble

No. of players   2 per drill group.

Distance   A to B—5 to 10 yards, Flags—10 to 15 yards apart.

Explanation   A throws the ball high into the air to B. B heads the ball toward flag 1. A runs to flag 1 and collects the ball. He dribbles around flag 1 and dribbles back to his starting position in front of flag 3. A picks up the ball and throws it to B who heads the ball to flag 2. A runs to flag 2 and collects the ball. He dribbles around flag 2 and dribbles back to flag 3.

Purpose   Players practice heading, dribbling, and trapping. Players improve their muscular endurance and physical fitness.

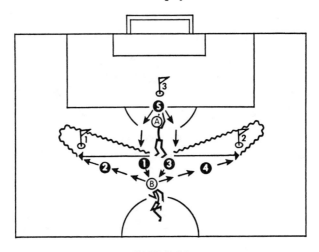

Drill 3–11

Flag Head, Trap, Dribble

Drill 3–12   Double Flag Circle and Outside-of-the-Foot Pass

No. of players   3 per drill group.

Equipment   2 flags—5 to 7 yards apart.

Explanation   A dribbles around (circles) the nearest flag and then around the second flag. A continues to dribble until he is alongside player B, as seen in the diagram. At this point, A square passes, using the outside-of-the-foot pass to player B. A then gets into the back of B's line. B repeats this same procedure and ends up by getting into the back of A's line.

Purpose   Players practice dribbling, feinting, and square passing. The square pass is made with the outside of the foot.

Variation   Same drill with 2 balls. Start one ball at position A and one at position B.

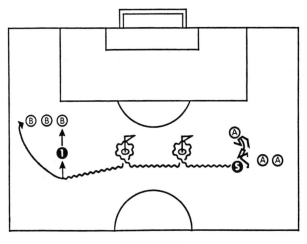

Drill 3–12

Double Flag Circle and Outside-of-the-foot Pass

Drill 3–13   Over the Head and Over the Flags

No. of players   6 per drill group.

Equipment   2 flags—2 yards apart.

Distance   A and B to the nearest flag—10 to 15 yards.

Explanation   A dribbles toward the nearest flag, turns 180 degrees, picks the ball up with his foot, flicks it over his head and over the flags. He then sprints to gather and control the ball. A then dribbles alongside player B, as seen in the diagram. At this point, A square passes, using the outside-of-the-foot pass to player B. A then gets on the end of B's line. B repeats this same procedure and ends up getting on the back of A's line.

Variation   Use 2 balls. Start one at position A and the other at position B.

Purpose   Players practice dribbling, feinting, over-the-head kicking, controlling, and square passing. The square pass is made with the outside of the foot.

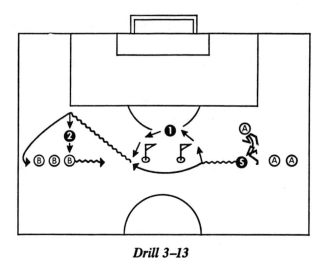

Drill 3–13

Over the Head and Over the Flags

Drill 3–14   Wing Feint Drill

No. of players   2 per drill group.

Distance   Flags to the side line—1 to 2 yards.

Equipment   5 flags, 1 ball per player

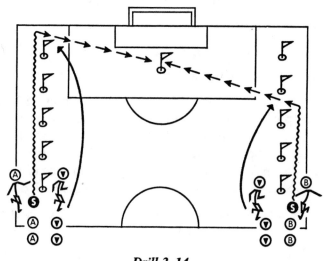

Drill 3–14

Wing Feint Drills

Explanation   Players A and B dribble down the touchlines, A on the right side and B on the left side. A and B must stay in the area marked off by the flags. A and B try to get clear of the defensive players, in order to cross the ball to the flag located in the penalty area. Defense players are not permitted inside the area marked off by the flags. The defensive players try to block the pathway of a crossed ball by staying between the target flag and player A or B.

Purpose   The main emphasis in this drill is to provide a setting for players A and B to practice change-of-pace runs, and other feigning techniques necessary for wing forwards to get clear to cross a ball. Defensive players practice getting into the proper position to cut off possible crosses or penetrating passes.

Drill 3–15   Dribble and Stop

No. of players   1 per drill exercise.

Distance   A to the end line—18 to 20 yards.

Explanation   Starting with player A, each player dribbles to each corner of the 18-yard line, then to each corner of the goal area. Finally, A dribbles to the left corner of the field, where A passes the ball to the next player in line, who repeats the same procedure. Players follow the numbers seen in the diagram. Each player must bring his ball to a complete

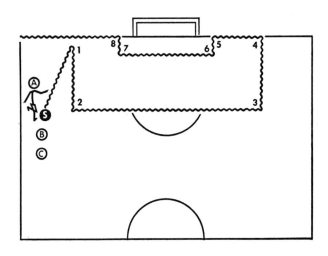

Drill 3–15

Dribble and Stop

stop on each number of corner before continuing to the next number or corner.

Purpose   Players improve their dribbling and feinting skills.

Drill 3–16 Dribble and Leave it

No. of players   1 per exercise.

Distance   Station I to Station II—25 to 30 yards. Station II to Station III—25 to 30 yards.

Equipment   16 cones or flags, 1 stop watch.

Explanation   Before play is started, a ball is placed at stations I, II, and III. Player A dribbles to station I and stops his ball, picks up the new ball and dribbles it to station II, stops his ball, picks a new ball, and so on. The ball must come to a complete stop before a player can pick up the next ball and proceed to the next station. Players can be timed to add incentive to the drill.

Purpose   Players practice a speed-dribbling drill with an element of control added to the drill.

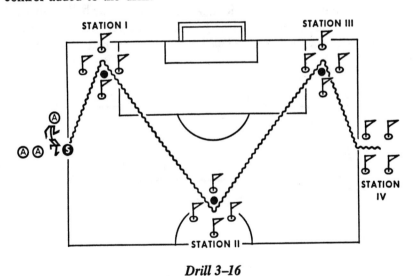

Drill 3–16

Dribble and Leave It

Drill 3–17 Drop-Off

No. of players   2 per drill contest.

Equipment   10 soccer balls.

Distance   A to B—30 to 40 yards.

Explanation   Each player starts with 5 balls. On a signal (whistle), players A and B dribble the ball to the center circle, then sprint back for another ball. The play is completed when a player drops off all 5 balls in the drop area, and the players involved run past the designated finish line.

Purpose   Each player in this drill will run approximately 350 yards. Therefore, this is an excellent drill for improving physical endurance and speed. Fast dribbling is practiced, yet the individuals should be instructed to control their movements.

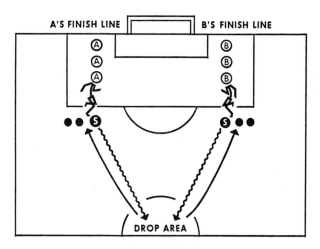

Drill 3–17

Drop Off

Drill 3–18   Pass Back or Go

No. of players   7 per drill group.

Distance   E to A, B, C, D,—5 to 10 yards.

Explanation   Players A, B, C, and D pass to E when he calls for the ball. E either passes back to the player who passes to him, or turns the ball and shoots at the goal. The defense player tries to prevent E from turning the ball. In starting the drill, players A, B, C, and D have a ball in front of them.

Purpose   The defensive player practices stopping E from turning a ball.

E practices turning and shooting a ball. E practices feinting to get the defensive player to commit himself. E tries to make the defensive player move in the wrong direction.

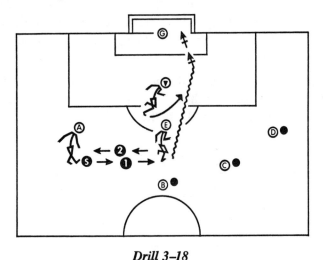

Drill 3–18

Pass Back or Go

Drill 3–19   Four Corner Dribble

No. of players   5 per drill group.

Distance   A, B, C, and D to the flag—10 yards.

Explanation   A dribbles to the center, turns the ball 360 degrees and passes off to player B. E steps into the square and takes the place that has been vacated by A. A then takes B's place and the drill is continued in the same manner.

Purpose   Players practice dribbling and turning the ball.

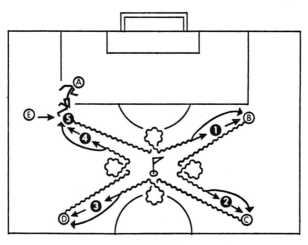

Drill 3–19

4 Corner Dribble

Chapter Four

Relating Shooting Drills to Match Play

The key to setting up shooting drills which relate to match play can be found in the word "variety." In match play, balls approach attacking players from every angle: from the front and the rear, from over the head and between the legs; they bounce high or low; they can curve, hook, drop, or rise; they can come in fast or slow. Attackers must sharpen their skills through a variety of shooting drills that develop agility and familiarize players with the varied challenges they will face in a match-play situation.

Opportunities for a shot on goal appear quickly and disappear just as quickly. From this we can see the need for instant reflexes to get the ball off fast before the opportunity is gone. One-touch shooting, therefore, is a necessity for a modern attacker.

In all shooting drills, accuracy over power and low shots over high shots should be stressed. Attackers should be encouraged to challenge defenders. This experience can be provided by a variety of one-on-one drills in the immediate area of the goal. It goes without saying that these drills should end up with a shot on goal.

Authorities recognize that high scorers remain calm under pressure and are not easily distracted. Hopefully, players will learn to cope with the distractions and concentrate on the task at hand. An example of such a drill is called "Hassle." In this drill, two defensive players are placed inside of the 18-yard line. They are about five yards apart and stand facing each other. Ten yards outside of the 18-yard line, attackers are stationed in a row. The coach rolls a ball between the two defense players, then one of the attackers runs between the defense and attempts a "one-touch" shot on the goal. The defense harasses the striker by running in front of him or by faking a kick at the ball. The defense players should do anything they can think of to distract or break the concentration of the striker. The only rule the defensive players must abide by is not to touch the ball or the striker. Even though this drill appears to be a simple task, because the defensive players are not allowed to touch the striker or the ball, many players at first cannot cope with the distractions. Many miss the ball completely. It is a good drill for all players and provides the ingredients that relate to the experiences and the pressure of match play.

It is said that "strikers are born and not made." This statement might well be true in some instances. But if it were completely true, there would be no need for strikers to practice their skills. Granted, certain physical qualities and personality types are necessary for a player to be an effective striker, but as coaches, it is important that we add the vital ingredients of experience and practice to these inborn qualities.

Drill 4–1 Full-Speed Shooting (No Diagram)

No. of players   2 per drill group.

Distance   A to the half-field line—5 to 10 (starting position).

Explanation   Player A runs full speed toward the goal while carrying a soccer ball in his hands. When he approaches the 18-yard line, he throws the ball into the air, approximately 10 feet in front of himself. A then kicks the ball at the goal before it hits the ground.

Purpose   Players practice kicking at the goal while running full speed.

Variation   Player A juggles the ball once or twice before he shoots at the goal.

Drill 4–2 Shot Calling (No Diagram)

No. of players   1. per exercise.

Distance   A to the half-field line—5 to 7 yards (starting position).

Explanation   Player A dribbles the ball toward the goal. When he reaches the 18-yard line, the coach yells out which corner the shot should be aimed at. The shot should be taken immediately. Example: "Right lower," "Right upper," "Left lower," "Left upper," "Upper middle," "Lower middle."

Purpose   Players practice accurate shooting. A coach can use this drill to discover which players are the accurate shooters on his team.

Drill 4-3   Rebound

No. of players   1 per drill exercise.

Equipment   1 bench or backboard.

Distance   A's pass-off point to the board—5 to 10 yards.

Explanation   A dribbles toward the 18-yard line. When A reaches the area where the bench or backboard is located, he rebounds the ball off the bench. The drill is ended with a shot at the goal.

Purpose   The primary purpose of this drill is to practice shooting at the goal after receiving a wall pass.

Variation   Add a series of benches for wall passing down one side of the field.

Variation   Place 2 benches 15 yards apart on the field, one to A's left,

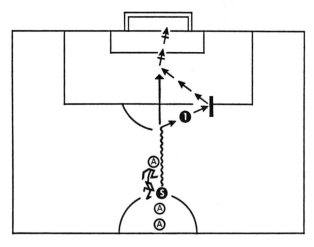

Drill 4-3

Rebound

around mid-field, and one further down the field, just outside the 18-yard line, to A's right. A must first make a wall pass to his left and then a wall pass to his right. The drill is completed with a shot on goal.

Drill 4–4 Forward Roll (No Diagram)

No. of players 1 per drill exercise.

Distance Starting position: A to half-field line—5 to 10 yards.

Explanation Carrying a ball in his hands, player A runs toward the goal. When he reaches the 18-yard line, he throws the ball ahead of himself, performs a forward roll, gets back to his feet, and immediately attempts a shot at the goal.

Purpose Players practice recovering their equilibrium. In other words, players learn to recover after falling or after being bumped by a defensive player.

Drill 4–5 Flick Over the Head (No Diagram)

No. of players 2 per drill group.

Distance A to B—3 yards.

Explanation B runs toward the goal. A lofts the ball slightly behind player B. B tries to flick the ball over his own head with the outside of his foot or with his heel. This procedure will enable him to get the ball in front of him. The drill is ended with a shot on goal.

Purpose Players practice a skill that will help them beat a defender and get free for a shot at the goal.

Drill 4–6 Volley Shooting (No Diagram)

No. of players 2 per drill group.

Distance A to G—5 to 7 yards. The goalkeeper centers himself in front of the goal-area line. The shooter, A centers himself in front of the 18-yard line.

Explanation The goalkeeper throws a ball 10 feet into the air toward player A. As soon as the goalkeeper throws the ball, he retreats in an attempt to stop A's volley shot at the goal.

Purpose Player A practices volley shooting while the goalkeeper practices retreating to stop a score.

Caution. Only volley shooting is permitted in this drill in order to protect the goalkeeper.

Drill 4–7 Turn and Shoot Around the Flags

No. of players   2 per drill group.

Distance   B to the flags—1 to 2 yards, A to B—4 to 6 yards.

Explanation   A passes to B. B pushes the ball outside the flags and shoots at the goal. B changes places with A, and the drill is repeated.

Purpose   Players practice turning a ball and shooting.

Variation   Eliminate the flags and introduce a defender into the drill.

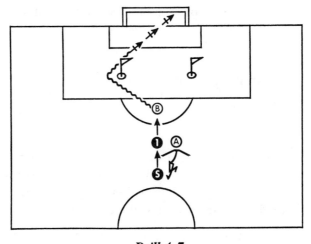

Drill 4–7

Turn and Shoot Around the Flags

Drill 4–8 Back Kicking (No Diagram)

No. of players   4 per drill group.

Distance   A to B, C, and D—6 to 10 yards.

Equipment   A has a supply of soccer balls.

Explanation   B, C, and D face player A. B, C, and D are standing on the front part of the goal-area line. A is facing B, C, and D while standing on the 18-yard line. A throws a ball higher than the waist of B, C, and D. Players attempt to take a shot at the goal by kicking the ball over their heads.

Purpose Players practice over-the-head kicking and shooting.

Drill 4–9 Hassle

No. of players 4 per drill group.

Distance Defensive players—5 yards apart. Offensive players line up outside the 18-yard line.

Equipment A has a supply of soccer balls.

Explanation A throws a ball between the 2 defensive players. B runs forward and attempts to shoot at the goal. The defensive player runs in front of the ball or does anything he can to harass player B's attempts to shoot at the goal. Defensive players are not allowed to touch player B or the ball.

Purpose Players learn to concentrate on the ball when being harassed, and learn to handle the ball in crowded areas.

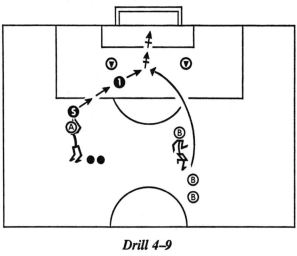

Drill 4–9

Hassle

Drill 4–10 Shoulder to Shoulder

No. of players 3 per drill group.

Distance A to B—10 to 15 yards, B to the defensive player—shoulder to shoulder.

Equipment Supply of soccer balls.

Explanation   B and the defensive player stand shoulder to shoulder facing away from the goal on the left side of the field, as seen in the diagram. A throws a ball and whistles to signal for play to start. B and the defensive player turn on the signal and attempt to get control of the ball. The defensive player is instructed to get the inside position, that is, to get his body between the goal and player B. B's objective is to get a shot at the goal, and the defensive player's objective is to turn the ball and to dribble it over the center line.

Purpose   The primary purpose of this drill is to practice quick shooting under pressure. Defensive players practice clearing a ball.

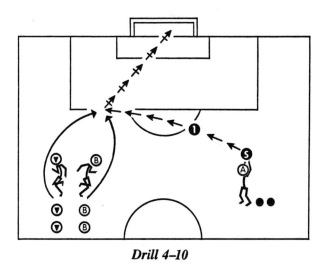

Drill 4–10

Shoulder to Shoulder

Drill 4–11   Push Thru

No. of players   4 per drill group.

Distance   A to the defensive player—3 to 5 yards.

Explanation   A throws the ball behind the 2 defensive players. Player B runs through the 2 defensive players chasing the ball and attempts to take a shot at the goal. Defensive players harass player B as he passes through. Defensive players should be careful not to injure player B. Harassment should be mild, such as a nudge or a slight bump. B is instructed to shoot the ball as soon as he approaches it.

Purpose   Players practice shooting under adverse conditions.

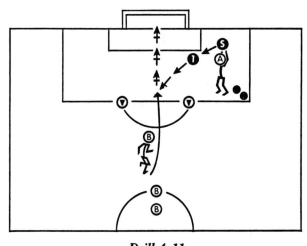

Drill 4–11

Push Thru

Drill 4–12   Around the Flag

No. of players   2 per drill group.

Distance   A to the flags—20 to 25 yards, defensive player to the flags—10 to 15 yards.

Equipment   1 flag or 1 cone.

Explanation   Player A dribbles a ball toward the flag. Just as A gets

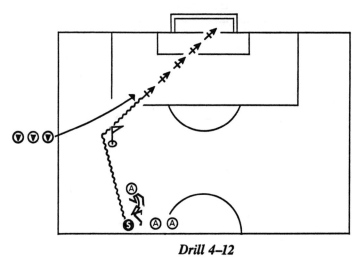

Drill 4–12

Around the Flag

close to the flag, the coach blows a whistle for the defensive player to come on the field and attempt to stop player A. A must stay to the left of the flag until he passes the flag. Then he cuts toward the goal. The pressure put on by the defensive player can be adjusted by moving the flag closer to or further away from the touchline. The defensive player is instructed to get the inside position, that is, to get his body between the goal and player A.

Purpose   Players practice dribbling, feinting, and shooting.

Variation   Use the other side of the field.

Drill 4–13   Gap Space

No. of players   9 per drill group.

Distance   D to C—5 to 10 yards, C to B—5 to 10 yards.

Explanation   Player A dribbles and feints to get clear to make a through pass to the open space behind B, C, or D. The player receiving the pass either shoots at the goal or passes off to a teammate who shoots at the goal.

Purpose   The primary purpose is for players to practice shooting at the goal under pressure from the defensive players.

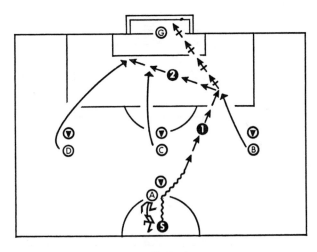

Drill 4–13

Gap Space

Drill 4–14   Speed and Endurance

No. of Players   5 per drill group

Distances   A to B—3 to 5 yards, A to E—15 to 20 yards, A to C—20 to 25 yards, A to D—15 to 20 yards.

Equipment   C supply of soccer balls, A, D, E each have a ball.

Explanation   Play is started when B receives a pass from A. B dribbles inside the penalty area and takes a shot at the goal. C then throws out another ball into the penalty restraining arc area, where B collects the ball, dribbles it and passes to player A. After passing, B receives another ball chest high, from D, traps the ball with his chest and immediately plays the ball back to D with his foot. B continues toward mid-field where he receives a high-lobbed pass from E. B heads back to E, then runs back to the start of the drill. Repeat this drill according to the physical condition of the players. Start with 3 times around.

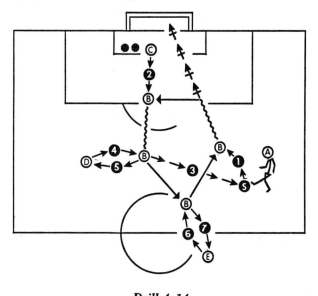

Drill 4–14

Speed and Endurance

Drill 4–15   Cross Runs and Cross Passes

No. of players   2 per drill group.

Distance   A to B—15 yards apart facing the goal.

Equipment   2 soccer balls.

Explanation   Player A and player B, each player makes a diagonal run to pick up the pass of the other player. Each player attempts a shot at the goal.

Purpose   Players practice passing to the space and not to the man.

Variation   Players pass the ball diagonally and run straight ahead to receive the pass. Then each player attempts a shot at the goal.

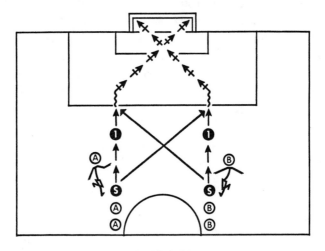

Drill 4–15

Cross Runs and Cross Passes

Drill 4–16   Exchange Dribbles Pass and Shoot

No. of players   2 per drill group.

Distance   A to B—10 to 15 yards.

Explanation   On a whistle signal, A and B exchange the ball. Each player controls the ball kicked to him and dribbles forward to the 18-yard line, at which point both send a lead pass diagonally across to the space in front of the other player, A to B and B to A. Each player sprints to the ball and shoots at the far corner of the goal.

Purpose   Players practice trapping, passing, dribbling, and shooting while progressing down the field.

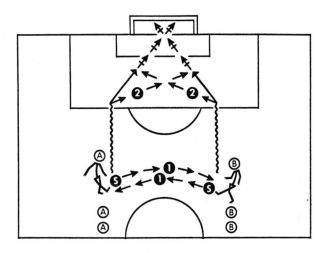

Drill 4–16

Exchange Dribble Pass and Shoot

Drill 4–17 Flag Shooting Drill

No. of players 1 per drill exercise.

Equipment 4 soccer balls and 1 flag.

Distance A to the flag—10 to 15 yards. The 4 balls are placed evenly on

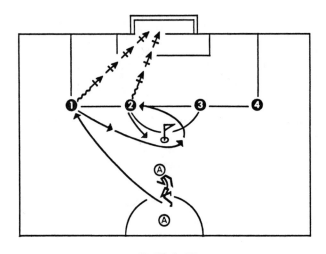

Drill 4–17

Flag Shooting Drill

the 18-yard line. (See diagram for the location of the 4 balls.) The flag is placed outside the 18-yard restraining arc.

Explanation   Player A sprints to the first ball to his left and shoots the ball at the goal. A then runs around the cone and heads for the second ball in the line. Repeat this procedure till all 4 balls have been shot at the goal. Emphasize getting the shot off quickly.

Purpose   Players practice shooting at the goal while they are improving their physical fitness.

Variation   Players dribble the ball to the goal area before a shot is taken.

Drill 4–18   Right and Left Pressure Shooting

No. of players   3 per drill group.

Distance   A to B—10 to 12 yards, A to C—10 to 12 yards.

Equipment   8 soccer balls and 1 flag.

Explanation   A and C have 4 balls each. A and C alternate serving balls to B until all 8 balls are exhausted. Each time B shoots at the goal, he runs around the flag. All shots are taken on a "one-touch" basis. Players change positions after each round of 8 balls. Defensive players can be added to this drill to create passive resistance to player B's attempts.

Purpose   This is a pressure shooting and a conditioning drill.

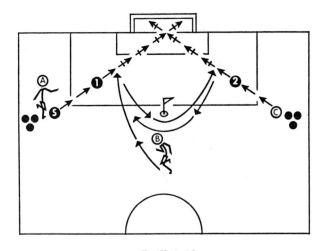

Drill 4–18

Right and Left Pressure Shooting

Drill 4–19 Step Over

No. of players   3 per drill group.

Distance   A to B—5 to 7 yards, B to C—5 to 7 yards.

Explanation   A passes across the penalty area. B steps over the ball while faking a kick at the ball. C shoots at the goal. C uses a "one-touch" shooting technique.

Purpose   Player C practices "one-touch" shooting after player B steps over the ball.

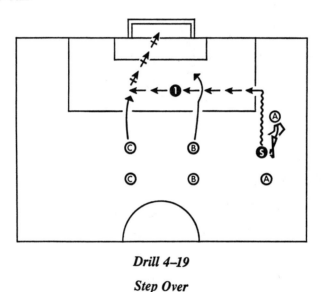

Drill 4–19

Step Over

Drill 4–20 Breakaway

No. of players   5 per drill group.

Distance   A, B, and C—5 yards apart.

Explanation   A starts the play on a signal by dribbling straight ahead. When he approaches the 18-yard line, he veers to his right and passes off to player C. B circles back to receive a pass from C. B shoots at the goal. Defensive players attempt to get ahead of the play and break it up, clearing the ball.

Purpose   Players practice fast-break maneuvers. Defensive players practice clearing a ball.

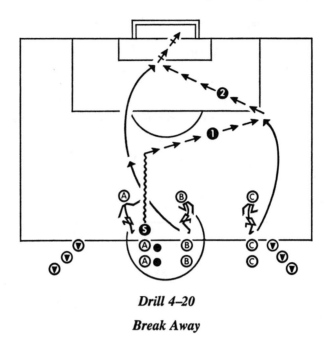

Drill 4–20

Break Away

Drill 4–21   Down the Line

No. of players   5 per drill group.

Distance   A, B, C and D—5 yards apart in a line, as seen in the diagram.

Explanation   In turn, players A, B, C, and D throw a ball to player E,

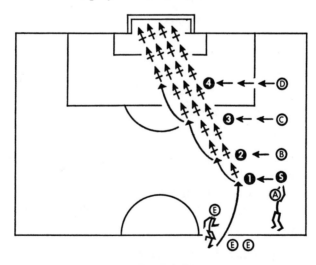

Drill 4–21

Down the Line

who shoots at the goal as soon as the ball arrives. E continues on the line until all 4 balls are shot at the goal.

Purpose Player B practices rapid shooting at various distances.

Drill 4–22 Pressure Shooting

No. of players 5 per drill group.

Distance E to the flag—5 yards.

Equipment 8 soccer balls and one flag.

Explanation E receives a pass from A. E then immediately shoots at the goal and runs around the flag, immediately receiving a pass from B, and so on. A, B, C, and D each have 2 balls. E repeats the entire cycle 2 times.

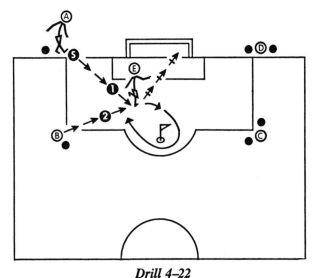

Drill 4–22

Pressure Shooting

Purpose This drill helps players to get off a shot at the goal quickly. Players improve their muscular endurance.

Variation Player E alternates shooting and passing back to the player who passes to him. Example: A passes the first ball, and E shoots it at the goal. B passes the second ball, and E passes it back to B. C passes the third ball, and E shoots it at the goal, and so on.

Drill 4–23 Speed Accurate Shooting

No. of players 1 per drill exercise.

Distance   A to the first ball—3 yards.

Equipment   9 soccer balls.

Explanation   9 soccer balls are placed on various spots of the 18-yard line and on the goal area line, as seen on the diagram below. Player A is timed to see how long it will take him to get all 9 balls into the goal. If a shot is missed, player A must retrieve the ball and shoot till it is in the goal. Player A must shoot the balls in the order shown in the diagram.

Purpose   Players practice rapid shooting without sacrificing accuracy.

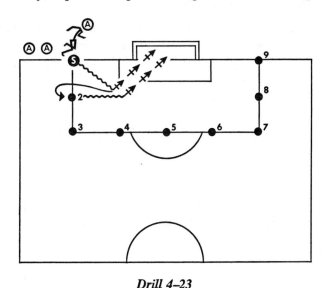

Drill 4–23

Speed Accurate Shooting

Drill 4–24   Daylight

No. of players   4 per drill group.

Distance   B and C to the defensive player—3 to 5 yards.

Explanation   A throws a ball in the vicinity of player B and C. The defensive player tries to keep players B and C surrounded. Players B and C look for daylight by dribbling to get clear for a shot at the goal. No wild kicking is allowed in this drill.

Purpose   Players practice quick shooting and ball control in close and congested areas.

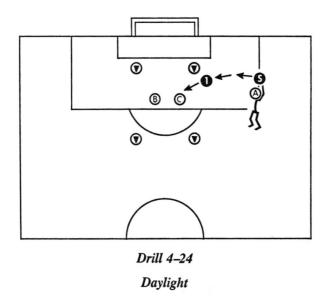

Drill 4–24

Daylight

Drill 4–25   Follow-Up Drill (No Diagram)

No. of players   2 per drill group.

Distance   A to half-field line—5 to 10 yards.

Explanation   A dribbles toward the penalty area. When he crosses the 18-yard line, he immediately takes a shot at the goal. If the goalkeeper catches the ball, he pushes it forward in any direction. Player A must follow up his shot. Change A's starting position so that he receives practice shooting at the goal from various angles.

Purpose   Players practice following up their shots at the goal.

Drill 4–26   Back Pass "One-Touch" Shooting (No Diagram)

No. of players   2 per drill group.

Distance   B to the penalty area arc—1 yard behind this half-circle.

Explanation   A has a supply of soccer balls. A back passes to B. Using a "1-touch" technique, B attempts to shoot at the goal. Change B's starting position so that he receives practice shooting at the goal from various angles.

Purpose   Players practice "1-touch" shooting after receiving a back pass.

Chapter Five

Relating Defense and Tackling Drills to Match Play

Regardless of what defensive system is used, zonal marking, man-for-man, sweeper, or a combination of these systems, certain techniques and tactics are common for these defense-related arrangements. The techniques and tactics can be practiced by using drills designed specifically to accomplish this purpose. All players should participate in these drills.

The following were the basis for developing defense and tackling drills:

1. Tackling technique drills—Basic tackling drills in which the tackler approaches from all sides.

2. Jockeying drills—These constitute a technique used to keep pressure on the opponent by being close enough for the pressure to develop, but remaining far enough away to keep from being tricked or easily beaten. This technique is used when the defensive player slides along with the offensive player until the offensive player makes a mistake. At this time, the tackle is attempted. It is also used to force the opponent into a certain area of the field that will put him at a disadvantage.

3. Sweeping drills—Drills designed to give players experience in backing each other up.

4. Drills designed to prepare the defense for blind side runs and quick switching of the ball from one side of the field to the other.

5. Funneling and moving out drills. As the ball moves toward the goal, the defense pulls closer together to prevent a score. If the ball is intercepted, the defense must move out quickly and spread out to reestablish width.

6. Drills that give players practice at quickly setting up a defensive system. This system should incorporate sound principles of balance, depth, and width.

7. Drills limiting passing opportunities by forcing opponents to shoot from unproductive angles and to kick with their weak feet.

8. Drills which concern quick clearing and quick counter-attacks.

9. Drills for more efficient communications with other players and especially with the goalkeeper.

10. Drills for causing the opponents to delay an attack—Forcing the opponents to make square and back passes, and preventing the through pass, which could speed up the attack.

The ten preceding ingredients are the basis of developing and selecting the drills in this chapter. Some of the drills, especially the technique drills, incorporate one or two phases of a defense. Others involve all ten and simulate a match play-situation.

Drill 5–1   Beat to the Ball (No Diagram)

No. of players   2 per drill group.

Distance   Starting position: A and the defensive player on opposite ends of the short side of the penalty area. A to the defensive player—40 to 45 yards apart.

Explanation   The ball is placed in the center of the penalty area. On a signal, player A and the defensive player sprint to get control of the ball. The defensive player tries to clear the ball up the field, and A tries to dribble the ball back to his starting position. Player A must stay within the penalty-area lines.

Purpose   Players practice tackling and digging a ball out. Players improve their speed in a one-on-one situation.

Drill 5–2   Defense Stop

No. of players   3 per drill group.

Distance   A to the defensive player—30 to 35 yards.

Explanation   The defensive player starts the drill by kicking the ball to the center circle. Player A gathers the ball and dribbles forward to the 18-yard line. If the defense player gets possession of the ball, play is started again by the next two players in each line. If player A beats the defensive player and is able to get the ball into the penalty area, the goalkeeper comes out and tries to stop player A. In this drill, no shooting at the goal is permitted. In order to score, player A must dribble over the goal line. If a defensive player cannot stop player A, the goalkeeper must take over.

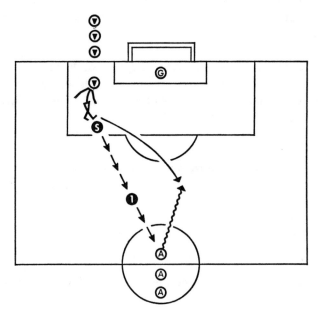

Drill 5–2

Defense Stop

Purpose The primary purpose of this drill is the practicing of tackling skills by the defensive player and the goalkeeper. The secondary purpose is to practice dribbling skills.

Drill 5–3 Defense Adjustment

No. of players 8 per drill group.

Explanation The ball is started from various offensive positions. This drill is played like a regular scrimmage (four-on-four). Offensive players (A's) try to score a goal, and the defensive players try to get control of the ball and return it to the other half of the field. On a signal, play is started. The four defensive players fall back and stagger the defense. As the defensive players fall back, they must adjust their positions according to the position of the ball. Players should not fall back one beside the other. The closest defensive player marks the man with the ball, while the others move deeper into defensive territory.

Purpose This drill helps players set up a defense and slow down the offense.

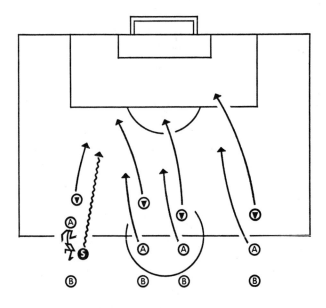

Drill 5–3

Defense Adjustment

Drill 5–4   Come Around

No. of players   4 per drill group.

Distance   B to C—10 to 15 yards.

Explanation   B and C only move laterally between the confines of the flags. A must free himself so that he can make a pass to players B or C. When A loses the ball to the defender, the players change roles. The objective is to make as many passes as one can without having the ball intercepted. A can pass either to B or C.

Purpose   Defensive players practice defensive skills, and offensive players practice protecting the ball.

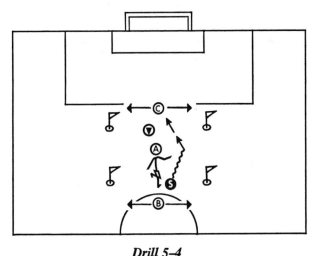

Drill 5–4

Come Around

Drill 5–5   Face Away—Cross the Line

No. of players   2 per drill group.

Distance   Cones are 5 yards apart.

Explanation   A, with his back to B, tries to dribble the ball to B's side of the line. B cannot cross the line to get the ball. He can only attack the ball when it is on his side of the two cones. Play is stopped when B gets behind A.

Purpose   Player A practices feinting while facing away from the defender. Player B practices defensive skills.

Variation   Player A starts while facing player B.

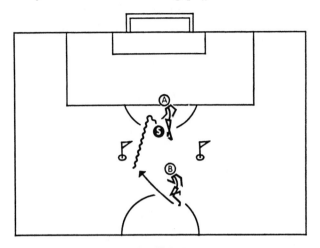

Drill 5–5

Face Away–Cross the Line

Drill 5–6   Rapid Clearing

No. of players   6 per drill group.

Distance   A, B, C, D, and E to the defensive player—40 to 50 yards.

Explanation   Players A, B, C, D, and E kick balls at the goal, one at a

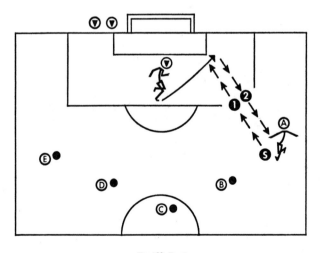

Drill 5–6

Rapid Clearing

time. The defensive player clears the balls up the field. As soon as the defender clears a ball, the next ball should be on its way in order to keep pressure on the defender. Afer 5 balls are cleared, a new defender comes on the field to perform.

Purpose   Defenders practice clearing balls under pressure.

Variation   Add an opposing player to the drill. This player should play in the same area as that of the defending player. The extra player tries to shoot the ball at the goal when he gets control of it.

Drill 5–7   Team Defense Recovery—1

No. of players   2 full teams.

Explanation   A throws to player B. This is the signal for all players on the defensive team to retreat and set up a defense. Player B, who has the ball, dribbles straight ahead. The defensive players nearest the ball and nearest to player B are encouraged to harass and slow player B down.

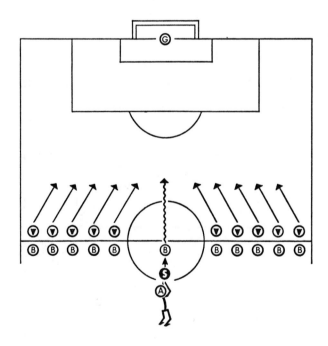

Drill 5–7

Team Defense Recovery—I

Drill 5–8   Team Defense Recovery—2

No. of players   2 full teams.

Explanation   A starts the play by dribbling down the field when a whistle is blown. The defensive team has two objectives: to slow the ball down, and to set up a defensive formation quickly on the far half of the field.

Purpose   Players learn to set up a defense quickly.

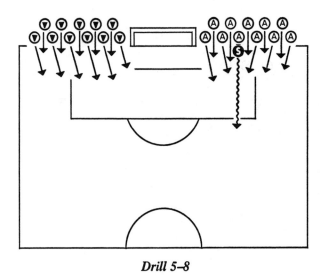

Drill 5–8

Team Defense Recovery—II

Drill 5–9   Team Defense Recovery—3

No. of players   8 per drill group.

Distance   A to B—15 to 20 yards, B to C—5 yards.

Explanation   On a whistle signal, offensive player A passes to B. B passes to C. In the meantime, the defense attempts to set up as indicated in the diagram. Each defensive player sweeps for the next player to his left. The last defensive player in the line watches for a sudden change or pass to D on the other side of the field. If a ball is crossed to the other side of the field, the sweeping order is reversed.

Purpose   Players practice backing each other up.

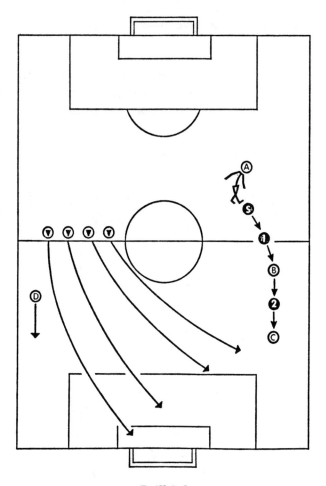

Drill 5–9

Team Defense Recovery—III

Drill 5–10   One-on-One Clearing

No. of players   6 or more.

Equipment   6 flags or cones.

Explanation   A tries to dribble past the first defensive player. If A suc-
ceeds, he proceeds to take on the second defensive player, and so on. If
the defender gains possession or clears the ball, the dribbler gets at the
end of the defender's line and becomes a defender. The tackler gets at the
end of the dribblers' line, and the other players move up one position.

Purpose Players practice tackling and dribbling in a one-on-one situation in a confined area.

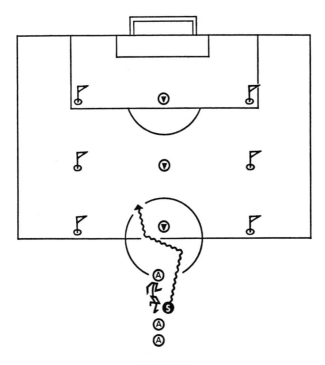

Drill 5–10

1 on 1 Clearing

Drill 5–11 Musical Balls

No. of players 5 per drill group.

Equipment 4 soccer balls.

Explanation 5 players line up on the 6-yard line. Four balls are placed in front of the center circle. On a signal, players race to get control of a ball. The player that does not get a ball attempts to take a ball away from one of the other players until the coach blows the whistle. Play continues for about one minute. Play is confined to half of the field.

Purpose Players improve their speed by trying to beat the other players to the ball. Players practice quick control and quick placement of a ball into a safe area.

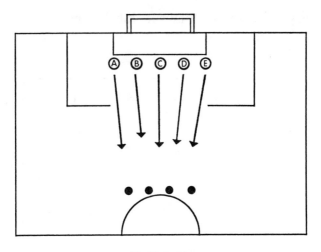

Drill 5–11

Musical Balls

Drill 5–12   Beat to the Ball

No. of players   8 per drill group.

Equipment   4 soccer balls placed at half-field, 15 yards apart.

Explanation   On a whistle signal, players run in order to beat their opponents to the ball. Players then attempt to score on the goal at the opposite end of the field. When a player scores, he may return to help the other players score.

Purpose   The primary purpose of this drill is for players to practice tackling and beating an opponent to the ball. Players also improve their physical fitness.

Drill 5–13   Fullback Pressure

No. of players   3 per drill group.

Distance   A to the defensive player—4 to 6 yards. The flags are on the left side of the half-field line.

Explanation   Play is started when A throws a ball between players B and the closest defender. The ball should be rolled closer to the defensive player in order to provide an advantage for the defensive player. When the defensive player gets control of the ball, he immediately tries to

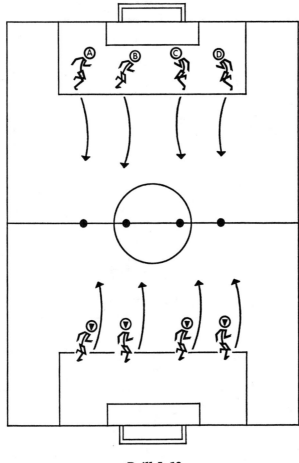

Drill 5–12

Beat To the Ball

dribble to the near touchline and to pass the ball down the field to the target flag.

Purpose   This drill is directed toward teaching defensive players to quickly get the ball to the outside of the field.

Drill 5–14   Target Shooting

No. of players   7 per drill group.

Explanation   Each offensive player (A, B, C, D, E, and F) has a soccer

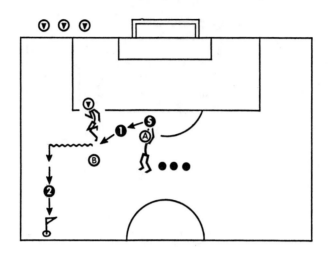

Drill 5–13

Fullback Pressure

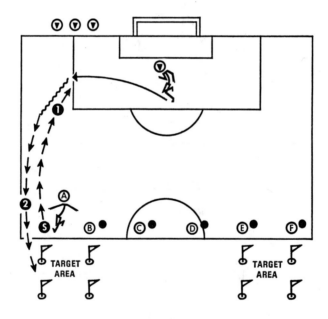

Drill 5–14

Target Shooting

ball. A starts the play by kicking his ball deep into the left corner. A defensive player recovers the ball, controls it, and attempts a long kick to the target area. As soon as the defensive man clears the ball, B kicks his ball down the field, and again the defensive player clears the ball to the target area. The drill continues, until all players have exhausted their soccer balls. A, B, C, D, E, and F are instructed to keep pressure on the defensive man. As soon as the defensive player clears a ball, the next ball should be on its way down the field.

Purpose Players practice long kicking under pressure. The defending player develops his muscular endurance.

Drill 5–15 Mark and Sweep

No. of players 4 per drill group.

Distance A to B—5 to 7 yards.

Explanation Each defensive player sweeps (backs up) for the other defensive player. When player A has possession of the ball, the closest defensive player marks him. When player A passes off to player B, the sweeper moves forward to mark player B, and the other defensive player becomes the sweeper. This procedure is repeated down the field. Only the player with the ball is marked or guarded.

Purpose This drill teaches defensive players how to stagger their defensive positions. Players learn how to mark a man (slow down) and how to back up a player (sweep).

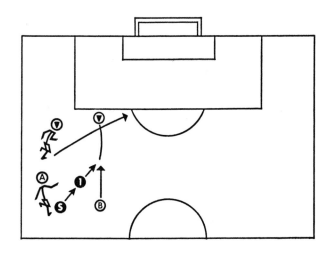

Drill 5–15

Mark and Sweep

Drill 5–16   Chase Drill

No. of players   2 per drill group.

Distance   A to the defensive player—1 yard. B to the defensive player—1 yard.

Explanation   Starting on the goal line, with the defensive player behind player A, a signal is given for play to start. The defensive player attempts to get the ball away from the offensive player before he reaches the half-field line. The objective of player A is to dribble over the half-field line.

Purpose   Defensive players practice recovering after they are beaten. Offensive players practice fast dribbling at full speed, while attempting to keep the defensive player behind them. Offensive players try to stay in the pathway of the defensive player.

Variation   Use 2 defenders.

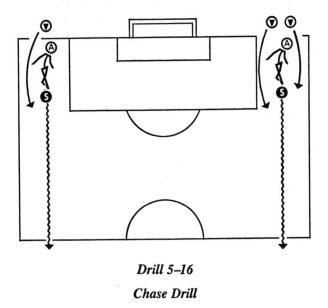

Drill 5–16

Chase Drill

Drill 5–17   Freedom (No Diagram)

No. of players   6 per drill group.

Distance   A on the 18-yard line facing the goal. B in front of A facing away from the goal. Each of these two players has a foot touching the ball.

Equipment   3 soccer balls.

Explanation   Play starts in the center of the penalty area. A is facing the goal, and the defensive player is facing away from the goal. The ball is placed between each defensive player and offensive player. Each player places his foot alongside of the ball. On a whistle signal, defensive players try to get the ball outside the penalty area. The offensive players try to get the ball in the goal.

Purpose   Defensive players get practice in playing in crowded areas, and also learn to mark closely.

Drill 5–18   Clear and Cross Behind

No. of players   8 per drill group.

Explanation   From outside of the 18-yard line, A players pass the ball toward the goal. The defensive players run out and stop the pass as quickly as possible. The defensive players control the ball, get it to the outside, and clear the ball to players B or C. Dribbling should be kept to a minimum. A players should keep the defenders moving. Immediately after clearing the ball, the defenders sprint behind the goal and change places. This drill is then repeated.

Purpose   Defenders practice clearing a ball. Defenders improve their muscular endurance.

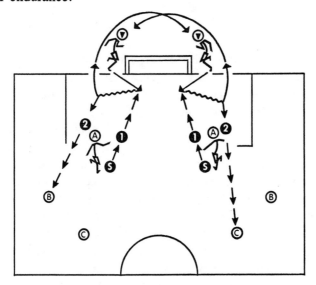

Drill 5–18

Clear and Cross Behind

Chapter Six

Relating Goalkeeping Drills to Match Play

Simply put, goalkeeper preparation involves keeping balls out of the goal, providing leadership for the defense, and starting the attack once the ball is won.

To keep balls out of the net, a goalkeeper needs frequent experience and drilling in catching, punching, and deflecting balls from every angle and from every height, traveling at various speeds and from various distances. Goalkeepers should be prepared to handle varied attempts upon the goal such as headed, lobbed, curving, rising, and falling balls.

A goalkeeper must know where to stand when he does not have the ball so that he can limit the opportunities of the opposing team. Diving for a ball and deflecting one over or around the goal post are emergency skills. A goalkeeper who is in the proper position before a shot is taken at the goal will not need to use these emergency skills as frequently as will a goalkeeper who is out of position. The proper position depends on the location of the shooter. The goalkeeper limits the opportunities of the shooter in two ways: (1) by moving across the face of the goal when the ball moves across the field, and (2) by moving out to meet an attacker to cut down the angle of possibility on a shot. A goalkeeper who is in the proper position may not appear as spectacular as one who is out of position, but he certainly will improve the team's chances of keeping the ball out of the goal.

Goalkeepers need the instincts and the intelligence to know when to come out for the ball, as well as when to remain in the goal. The first reason a goalkeeper comes out of the goal is to cut down the angle of possibility of a ball going into the goal. The closer the goalkeeper is to the attacker, the less the attacker will be able to see of the goal. In addition, the goalkeeper has a greater chance to deflect the ball over or around the goal post. The second reason a goalkeeper comes out of the goal is to place pressure on the attacker so that the attacker will become nervous and so possibly make a mistake.

From the preceding paragraphs, we can see that the training of goalkeepers requires much time, planning, and practice because his responsibilities are numerous. Meeting these responsibilities has a profound effect upon the outcome of a match-play situation. I feel that the best way to meet the challenge of these responsibilities is to separate them into parts so that they are easily understood. Once they are broken down, a drill can be planned to specifically duplicate the action of the responsibility. This way, hopefully, nothing is left unattended or to chance.

Drill 6–1   Goalkeeping Falling Drills (No Diagram)

No. of players   2 per drill group.

Distance   3 or 4 yards apart.

Explanation   Drill I—Goalkeeper receives balls to his left or to his right while in a sitting position. The ball is thrown so that the goalkeeper must fall in order to catch it.

Purpose   The goalkeeper practices diving and catching a ball. The above drill and the two variations of this drill are agility improvement drills.

Variation   The goalkeeper receives balls in a kneeling position.

Variation   The goalkeeper receives balls in a standing position.

Drill 6–2   Tennis Ball Drill (No Diagram)

No. of players   2 per drill group.

Distance   G to A—10 to 15 yards.

Equipment   A bag of tennis balls—20 to 30 balls.

Explanation   A throws tennis balls at G (the goalkeeper). The goal-keeper attempts to get out of the way of the thrown balls. The balls are thrown at a high rate of speed in a rapid-fire succession.

Purpose   Goalkeepers can develop their agility and ability to move quickly.

Variation   The goalkeeper catches the tennis balls instead of getting out of the way of them.

Drill 6–3   Reaction (No Diagram)

No. of players   2 per drill group.

Distance   A to G—4 to 8 yards.

Explanation   The goalkeeper faces the goal with his back to the field. A throws the ball at the goal and at the same time yells "ball." The goal-keeper turns and tries to save and catch the ball. A varies his throws in order to keep the goalkeeper guessing where the ball is going to be thrown.

Purpose   The main purpose of this drill is to improve the quickness and muscular endurance of the goalkeeper.

Variation   The goalkeeper faces the field with his back to the goal while A stands behind the goal. A loops the ball just over the goal post and, at the same time, A yells "Ball." The goalkeeper turns, runs to the ball, and taps it back over the goalpost.

Drill 6–4   2-Ball Throwback (No Diagram)

No. of players   2 per drill group.

Distance   A to the goalkeeper—10 yards.

Equipment   2 soccer balls.

Explanation   A throws the first ball to the right side of the goalkeeper. The goalkeeper catches it and immediately throws it back to A. As the goalkeeper is throwing the ball back to A, A throws the second ball to the left side of the goalkeeper. A should keep the goalkeeper moving. The goalkeeper returns the ball to player A at chest level. This procedure aids in keeping the balls moving at a rapid pace. The drill is continued until it is evident that the goalkeeper is physically slowing down.

Purpose   This drill is primarily used to improve the goalkeeper's muscular endurance.

Drill 6–5 Hard Throwing (No Diagram)

No. of players 2 per drill group.

Distance A to the goalkeeper—18 yards—14 yards—12 yards—8 yards.

Explanation A throws the ball at the goalkeeper from various distances. A throws the balls as hard as the goalkeeper can catch them. A throws a series of balls from each of the following distances—18 yards, 14 yards, 12 yards, and 8 yards. A throws each ball as near to the goalkeeper as possible.

Purpose This is practice for the goalkeeper to catch hard, fast shots at the goal.

Drill 6–6 Rebound

No. of players 2 per drill group.

Distance A to the goalkeeper—5 to 10 yards, the goalkeeper to the backboard—3 to 5 yards.

Equipment A backboard or any rebound surface.

Explanation The goalkeeper faces the backboard. A throws a ball at the backboard, and the goalkeeper catches the ball as it rebounds off of the wall or backboard. When the goalkeeper becomes accustomed to this drill, he moves closer to the backboard.

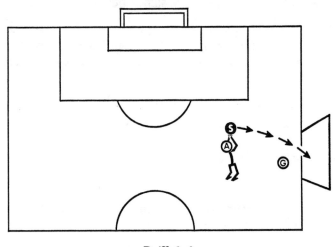

Drill 6–6

Rebound

Purpose The goalkeeper practices catching the rebounded balls. Further, he improves his ability to move quickly.

Variation The goalkeeper faces away from the backboard and turns to receive the rebounded balls.

Drill 6–7 Dunk (No Diagram)

No. of players 2 per drill group.

Distance A to the goalkeeper—12 to 15 yards.

Equipment 10 soccer balls.

Explanation A throws 10 soccer balls, one at a time to the goalkeeper. The first ball is thrown to the goalkeeper's left side, the second ball is thrown to his right side. When the goalkeeper catches the ball, he dunks (basketball style) over the goalpost. The goalkeeper then runs to the right corner of the goal and receives the second ball, which he dunks over the goalpost. This procedure is repeated until all 10 balls are thrown at the goalkeeper.

Purpose The purpose of this drill is to improve the agility and muscular endurance of the goalkeeper.

Drill 6–8 Volley Kick to the Goalkeeper

No. of players 3 per drill group.

Distance A to G—4 to 6 yards; A stands behind the goal.

Explanation A throws a ball over the goal post and B volley kicks the ball in an attempt to score a goal. The goalkeeper faces player B and is not permitted to turn around to see when or where the thrower (A) is throwing the ball.

Purpose The main purpose of this drill is to improve the goalkeeper's quickness. Player B practices volley kicking.

Drill 6–9 Forward Roll and Coming Out

No. of players 3 per drill group.

Distance See the diagram. A and B start on the spot where the 18-yard line and the goal line intersect.

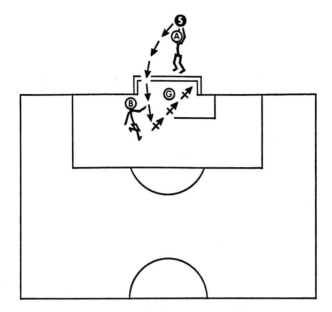

Drill 6–8

Volley Kick to the Goalkeeper

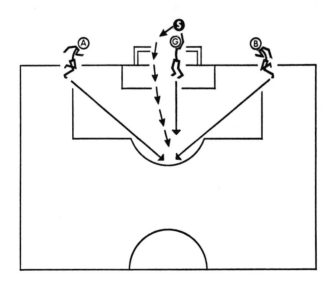

Drill 6–9

Forward Roll and Coming Out

Explanation The goalkeeper throws the ball to the penalty area restraining arc. As soon as the goalkeeper throws the ball, he executes a forward roll, then immediately chases after the ball. Players A and B try to beat the goalkeeper to the ball.

Purpose Goalkeepers practice coming out for a ball.

Drill 6–10 Surprise

No. of players 4 per drill group.

Distance G to A—10 yards, G to B—10 yards, G to C—10 yards.

Explanation A, B, and C throw a ball back and forth to each other. A, B, and C try to surprise the goalkeeper occasionally by quickly heading the ball at the goal, instead of catching it. The goalkeeper must follow the ball as the players pass it around the goal area.

Purpose The goalkeeper practices cutting down the angle of the shot, and the goalkeepers increase their quickness.

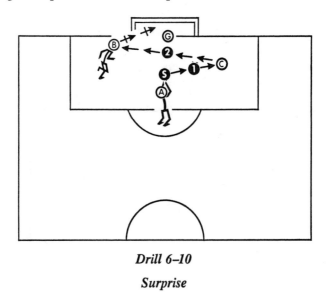

Drill 6–10

Surprise

Drill 6–11 Ricochet (No Diagram)

No. of players 4 per drill group.

Distance A to G—18 yards, A to B—18 to 20 yards, A to C—18 to 20 yards.

Equipment   Cones placed around and throughout the goal area.

Explanation   The players A, B, and C take turns shooting at the goal through the cones. When a ball hits a cone, the goalkeeper must adjust his position to accommodate the rebound and to catch or deflect the ball.

Purpose   The goalkeeper practices catching balls as they ricochet off the cones. This drill is used for improving a goalkeeper's quickness.

Variation   Players, instead of cones, to distract the goalkeeper.

Drill 6–12   Goalkeeper Dribble (No Diagram)

No. of players   2 per drill group.

Distance   A to G—18 yards.

Explanation   A shoots at the goal from the 18-yard line. The goalkeeper catches and tries to roll the ball forward to the edge of the 18-yard line. Player A tries to kick the ball away from the goalkeeper as he rolls the ball. Player A, when trying to kick the ball, should take care not to injure the goalkeeper. No wild kicking permitted in this drill.

Purpose   The goalkeeper practices rolling the ball to the edge of the 18-yard line under pressure of interception.

Drill 6–13   3 Goals

No. of players   5 per drill group.

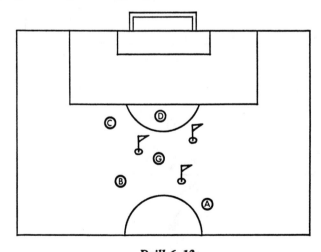

Drill 6–13

3 Goals

Equipment   3 flags or cones in a triangle formation. Each side of the triangle is 2 yards long.

Explanation   Players A, B, C, and D pass the ball around the 3 flags in order to find an opening to score a goal in one of the three goals. The goalkeeper adjusts his position depending upon where the ball is located. To score a goal, a player must pass the ball through the flags, at a level no higher than the goalkeeper's waist.

Purpose   The goalkeeper practices adjusting his position according to the position of the ball.

Drill 6–14   In and Out

No. of players   8 per drill group.

Explanation   2 soccer balls are placed inside of the middle of the center circle. Two goalkeepers stand at opposite positions outside the center circle. On a whistle signal, the goalkeepers race to see who can get a ball out of the center circle first. The three players in each half of the center circle can get in the way of the goalkeeper, but they cannot use their hands to keep the ball away from the goalkeeper. Once a goalkeeper gets

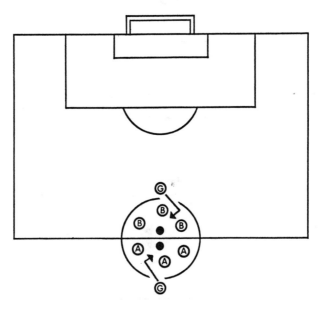

Drill 6–14

In and Out

possession of the ball, the 3 opposing players attempt to delay his return to the outside of the circle. The goalkeeper must get out of the circle on the same side that he entered it.

Purpose Goalkeepers practice moving in and out of crowded areas.

Caution All players should be cautioned not to get too rough in the execution of this drill.

Drill 6–15   Cutting the Angle (No Diagram)

No. of players 10 to 15 per drill group.

Equipment 1 ball per player.

Explanation Starting with player A, each player kicks his ball at the goal. The goalkeeper moves to the position best suited for him to save the shot. In other words, the goalkeeper protects the near post on angle shots, and positions himself near the middle of the goal when shots are coming from directly in front of the goal.

Purpose The goalkeeper practices adjusting his position to cut down the angle of the shot.

Variation The coach calls a random letter and the player with that letter dribbles 3 times and shoots at the goal. It is up to the goalkeeper to adjust his position as the player dribbles for a shot.

Drill 6–16   Coming Out (No Diagram)

No. of players 6 to 12 per drill group.

Equipment 1 ball per dribble.

Explanation Players attempt to dribble and keep their ball away from the goalkeeper. All players must stay within the penalty area. When a goalkeeper gets possession of a ball, he throws it out of the penalty area. This player must leave the penalty area. Play is continued until all players are eliminated by the goalkeeper.

Purpose Goalkeeper practices clearing balls out of the penalty area.

Caution Players should be cautioned to avoid dangerous and wild kicking.

Drill 6–17   Goalkeeper Mat Drill

No. of players 2 per drill group.

Distance   G to A—5 to 7 yards.

Equipment   2 gymnastic mats and 2 soccer balls.

Explanation   Two balls are placed next to the goalkeeper as shown in the diagram. A throws a ball first to the goalkeeper's left, and then one to the goalkeeper's right. The goalkeeper dives over the ball, catches it, and lands on his hip on the mats.

Purpose   Goalkeeper practices proper diving and landing techniques.

Variation   The balls on the mat are placed further away from the goalkeeper. After the goalkeeper successfully dives and retrieves the ball, the ball is moved 4 inches further away from the goalkeeper. The goalkeeper is not permitted to take a step before he dives for the ball.

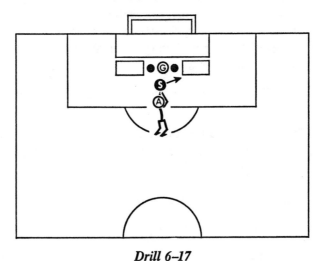

Drill 6–17

Goalkeeper Mat Drill

Drill 6–18   Chest and Shoot

No. of players   3 per drill group.

Distance   G to G—15 to 20 yards; G's to A—6 to 7 yards.

Equipment   4 cones or 4 flags.

Explanation   G (goalkeeper) throws a ball to A's chest. A traps the ball on his chest. A must turn the ball and shoot it between the cones behind him before the ball hits the ground. The ball must be kept below the goalkeeper's waist. A then repeats the same procedure facing the other goalkeeper.

Purpose   Goalkeepers practice stopping hard-kicked balls while player A practices chest traps, rapid shooting and turning a ball.

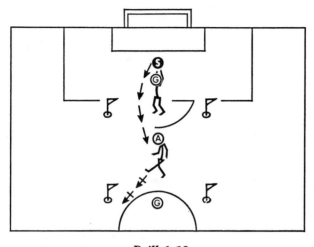

Drill 6–18

Chest and Shoot

Drill 6–19   Space Drill

No. of players   2 per drill group.

Distance   A to B—10 to 15 yards.

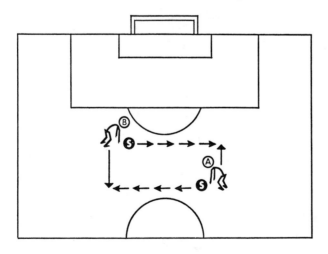

Drill 6–19

Space Drill

Equipment   2 soccer balls.

Explanation   On a whistle signal, goalkeepers A and B roll their balls straight ahead on the ground. Each player runs to receive the other player's ball. This same procedure is repeated for a period of 45 seconds.

Purpose   Goalkeepers practice various catching techniques. Goalkeepers improve their muscular endurance.

Variation   The players catch the ball baseball-style while kneeling on one knee.

Variation   The goalkeepers use bounce passes and practice catching high bounding balls.

Drill 6–20   Coming Out and Retreat

No. of players   2 per drill group.

Distance   A, the thrower, stands just outside the 18-yard line.

Explanation   A drops the first ball just inside the 18-yard line. The goalkeeper races out to pick it up. The goalkeeper immediately throws the ball back to A, who immediately lobs it over the goalkeeper's head. This ball is directed toward the goal, and the goalkeeper must get back to either punch or catch the returned ball. The drill is then repeated. The thrower (A) should keep the goalkeeper moving.

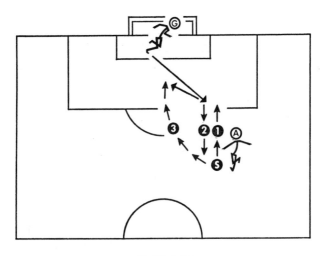

Drill 6–20

Coming Out and Retreat

Purpose The goalkeeper practices quick recovery skills, and coming out for the ball and retreating after a play is made.

Drill 6–21   Goalkeeper Score Game

No. of players   2 per drill group.

Distance   2 small goals, 15 yards apart.

Explanation   Players are not permitted to enter the neutral zone. They kick the ball from behind the neutral zone line. One goalkeeper kicks the ball at the other goalkeeper's goal, and the other goalkeeper attempts to keep the ball out of the goal. If the defending goalkeeper catches the ball and prevents it from scoring, he attempts to score by drop kicking at the opposite goal. If the defending goalkeeper causes a corner to be awarded, he loses his turn at kicking at the other goal. The game is continued until one goalkeeper kicks 5 successful goals.

Purpose   Goalkeepers practice protecting the goal against hard shots.

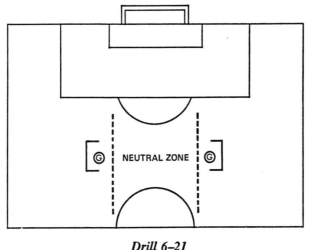

Drill 6–21

Goalkeeper Score Game

Drill 6–22   Push Around—Push Over

No. of players   3 per drill group.

Distance   A to the near post—10 to 15 yards; B is behind the goal, as seen in the diagram.

Equipment   A supply of soccer balls.

Explanation   A rolls a ball just outside the goal post. G (the Goalkeeper) dives to save the ball. The goalkeeper either catches it or punches the ball to the outside. B loops the next ball just over the goal post. The goalkeeper must push this second ball back over the goal post. This drill is then repeated.

Purpose   Players practice punching and catching balls. Goalkeepers improve their muscular endurance.

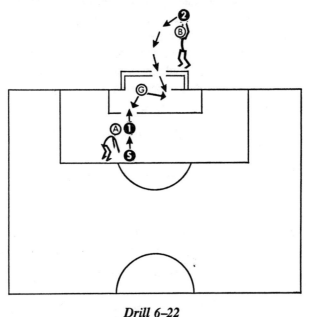

Drill 6–22

Push Around, Push Over

Drill 6–23   Find the Ball

No. of players   2 per drill group.

Distance   G to A—3 to 5 yards.

Explanation   A is walking backward dropping a ball in a random fashion. The goalkeeper performs a forward roll and comes back to his feet looking for the ball. The goalkeeper immediately dives to collect the ball, then throws the ball back to A and does a forward roll. The same procedure is then repeated. As the goalkeeper starts his forward roll, A drops the ball in the immediate area of the goalkeeper.

Purpose The goalkeeper develops agility and the ability to recover balls after being bumped or jostled.

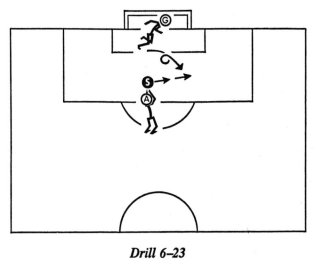

Drill 6–23

Find the Ball

Drill 6–24 Beat the Keeper

No. of players 3 per drill group.

Distance G on the goalline. A—halfway between the 18-yard line and the kickoff line. B on the kickoff line.

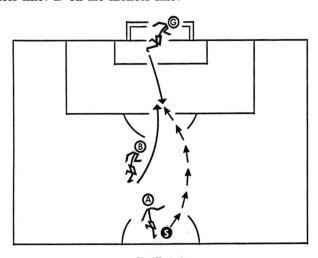

Drill 6–24

Beat the Keeper

Explanation   A kicks balls in the air between G and B. The goalkeeper must decide to advance or to hold his ground.

Purpose   Goalkeeper practices deciding whether to advance or to hold his ground.

Drill 6–25   Other Individual and Dual Activities for Goalkeepers (No Diagram)

1. The goalkeeper lies on his back. He throws a ball in the air, gets on his feet, and catches the ball before it hits the ground.
2. Two goalkeepers, 10 feet apart, facing each other, bounce-pass a ball back and forth. As a variation, the goalkeepers use two balls. One goalkeeper bounce-passes while the other goalkeeper chest passes.

Variation   Two players attempt to juggle three balls.

3. In a prone, arched position, the goalkeeper rocks up and down. Another goalkeeper throws balls in such a manner that the goalkeeper, still in the prone position, catches the ball when his head is at the highest position of the rocker arch.
4. Goalkeeper, on his knees, falls left or right with a ball in his hands. He must fall without using his hands to break the fall.
5. Goalkeeper rolls a ball between his legs, turns, and falls on or dives after the ball.
6. Two goalkeepers work together. One goalkeeper is face down on the 6-yard line; the other goalkeeper, standing on the center of the 18-yard line, rolls a ball toward the goal and yells ''Go.'' The goalkeeper on the ground must get up and chase the ball that the other goalkeeper has thrown toward the goal. The ball should be thrown in such a manner as to give the goalkeeper a chance to either catch it or dive on it.
7. From a crouched position, a goalkeeper springs to the side to catch thrown balls. The goalkeeper should attempt to remain on his feet after he springs for the ball. After the goalkeeper receives the ball, he throws the ball back and quickly assumes the crouched position to receive another ball.
8. Two goalkeepers sit facing each other, with their knees up and their feet touching. One goalkeeper hands the ball to the other goalkeeper. With the ball in his hands, he does a sit-up and hands the ball off to the other goalkeeper, who repeats the sit-up exercise.

9. Two goalkeepers sit facing each other, about 5 yards apart, and throw a ball back and forth. The ball should be thrown to one side, within the reach of the receiving goalkeeper in an attempt to make the receiving goalkeeper fall over to catch the ball.

10. The goalkeeper faces the corner of a two-sided backboard. Another goalkeeper throws a ball into the corner and the goalkeeper catches the rebound.

11. Set up targets for the goalkeeper to practice drop-kicking and punting. At mid-field, you can set up a 5-yard square with the cones or flags. Move the target around so that the goalkeeper gets practice at kicking to various areas of the field.

12. Two goalkeepers place their hands on a soccer ball. On a whistle signal they both try to get possession of the ball. The players wrestle with their hands on the ball until one of the two players gets sole possession of it.

Section Two

Basic Patterns

A game of soccer is one big battle made up of many little battles. If you win the majority of little battles, you are more likely to win the game. To win the small battles, step by step small-group tactical procedures have been established through the years to enable the small group to exploit the other team.

These tactical procedures are used to surprise, confuse, and exploit your opponent's mistakes and weaknesses. They also deny your opponent possession of the ball and enable you to utilize your strengths and minimize your weaknesses. In other words, these procedures are a means to take advantage of the situation at hand in an efficient, effective manner.

In this section of the book, you will find many small-group tactical drills. These are used to prepare players to become experienced in handling the following aspects of the game: how to support other players; how and when to make a wall pass and a give-and-go pass; how to use decoy, diagonal, overlapping, and crisscross runs; how to use square, diagonal, and back passes; when to dribble and when to pass off. Knowledge of and repeated practice in the execution of these procedures will provide an individual with the wide range of experiences necessary to handle various situations as they occur in a game.

When and how you use these drills depends upon the experience and maturity of your players. An adequate level of technique is necessary to be successful in performing these drills. The grid drills are used to reinforce technique. They can be used once an adequate level of technique is exhibited by the players involved.

In order to perform the moving passing drills and the small-group passing drills, a greater level of technique is needed than in performing the grid drills. If the moving passing drills and the small-group passing drills are introduced before a maturity of skills can be displayed, players will experience frustration and, subsequently, confusion. At this point in their training, they do not have the control necessary to carry out the skills that are needed to perform these drills. So it is better to put this part of the training off until further skill is evident.

Through participation in the exercises and patterns in this section, players are better able to anticipate each other's actions. They will learn to work together in small groups, and to contribute to the entire team's tactical goals of maintaining possession of the ball and scoring goals.

Players should get a chance to practice and perfect the tactical patterns they have learned in a scrimmage and/or in a small-sided game. During these games, you can help your players recognize opportunities as they develop. Use the small-group basic passing patterns that were learned and practiced in the drilling process.

Chapter Seven

Relating Grid Drills to Match Play

While practicing grid drills, players experience offensive and defensive pressure in a restricted area under realistic game-like situations. Grid drills are used to practice ball control and defensive techniques and tactics. The space in the grid is limited so that players will not be running all over the field. This insures that the players will experience frequent encounters and learn to use space efficiently and effectively. Another reason for limiting the space is to increase the pace of the action. The smaller the grid, the greater the need for quick passing, rapid trapping, and instant supporting. As the skill of the players improves in performing within the grids, decrease the size of the grid to increase the pressure and pace of the drill. If the players have difficulty performing in the grids, increase the size of the grid until their execution of the skill improves. In grids, two or more players can work together by using sound principles of movement and predetermined patterns of passing and supporting which have proven to be successful.

The value of "one-touch," short-passing on the ground plays can be easily seen and practiced in grids. Through repetition, players learn and develop techniques involving the correct exploitation of space and numerical superiority. In addition, confinement to the grids forces players to develop a greater sense of discipline than they would through drills alone.

For defensive players, the grid drills provide experiences in breaking up established passing patterns. They learn how to harass, when to delay the opponents, when to jockey, when to attempt the tackle, and when to attempt and win possession of the ball.

Because the action in grids is intense, physical conditioning is another bonus in this training procedure. Play inside the grid is continuous and demanding. Therefore, players improve their speed and endurance.

Grid drills can enable you to handle a large number of players in a limited space. In a field 100 yards long and 50 yards wide, you can set up 50 grids or squares, each grid being 10 yards by 10 yards. Further, because the action in the grid is confined, it is easy to oversee and to supervise the action.

Finally, grid drills are valuable tools in preparing players for the challenges they will meet in attacking and defending.

Drill 7–1   Grid Drills—One-on-One, Two-on-One, Three-on-One, Four-on-Two

No. of players   2, 3, 4, and 6 per drill group.

Distance   The drills are performed in a ten-yard square.

Equipment   4 flags or cones to mark off each 10-yard grid.

Explanation One-on-One   A dribbles inside the square, trying to shield the ball from the defensive player. When the defensive player clears the ball out of the square, the players change roles. B becomes the dribbler, and A becomes the defensive player.

Purpose   Players practice dribbling and tackling skills.

Two-on-One—Players A and B keep the ball away from the defensive player. When A has possession of the ball, player B must get into position to receive the ball.

Purpose   Players practice dribbling, controlling, and passing skills. This drill is specifically designed to teach players what to do when they are not in possession of the ball. This is called "running off the ball."

Three-on-One—Players A, B, and C pass the ball around the square in an attempt to keep the ball away from the defensive players.

Purpose   This drill is specifically designed to teach players how to support the player with the ball by providing two opportunities for the man with the ball to pass it to one of the other players.

Four-on-Two—Players A, B, C, and D pass the ball around and across the square, keeping the ball away from the defensive players.

Purpose   A pass made diagonally across the square is considered a penetrating pass. A game can be played whereby a diagonal pass across the square is a score. Players pass the ball around the square until a diagonal pass can be made.

Note: Inexperienced players may have trouble controlling the ball in a 10-yard square. In this case, the square can be made larger. Once the players have mastered the larger squares, they can go back and try the 10-yard squares again.

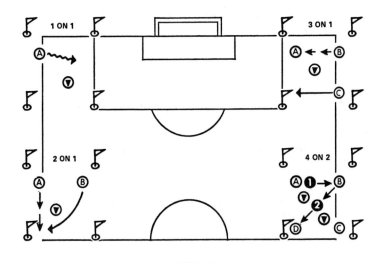

Drill 7–1

Grid Drills—1 on 1, 2 on 1, 3 on 1, 4 on 2

Drill 7–2   Four-on-Two—Stay on the Line

No. of players   6 per drill group.

Equipment   4 cones or flags for a 10 to 15-yard square.

Explanation Players A, B, C, and D pass the ball around and through the square. A, B, C, and D must stay on the perimeter of the square. The two defensive players try to get possession of the ball.

Purpose Players practice square passing in preparation for a through or a penetrating pass.

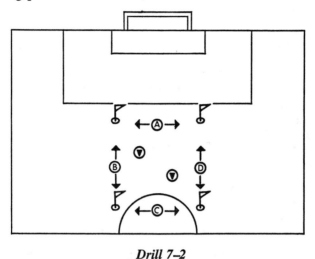

Drill 7–2

4 on 2—Stay on the Line

Drill 7–3   Speed Dribble—Random Dribble—Cue Ball—Kick Out

Speed Dribble (No Diagram)

No. of players 1 per drill.

Equipment 4 flags or cones to mark off a 10-yard square.

Explanation A dribbles inside the square for a period of 45 seconds. A is instructed to move quickly inside the square. After 45 seconds, another player takes his turn at dribbling inside the square.

Purpose Players practice dribbling, feinting, and controlling a ball.

Random Dribble (No Diagram)

No. of players As many as can dribble and move about inside a 10-yard square.

Equipment 1 ball per player, 4 flags per grid.

Explanation　Players dribble in and out of the other players inside the marked-off square.

Purpose　Players practice dribbling in crowded areas.

Cue Ball (No Diagram)

No. of players　3 per drill group.

Equipment　3 soccer balls, 4 flags to mark off a 10-yard square.

Explanation　Each of the three players has a ball. Player A protects his ball and attempts to keep it from being hit by either of the other defensive players' balls. After 45 seconds, one of the defending players changes roles with player A.

Purpose　This drill gives practice in dribbling, screening, and controlling a ball.

Kick Out (No Diagram)

No. of players　As many as can move in a 10-yard square.

Equipment　1 ball per player, 4 flags or cones to mark off the grid.

Explanation　Offensive players practice dribbling in crowded areas, and defensive players practice clearing balls as well as other tackling skills.

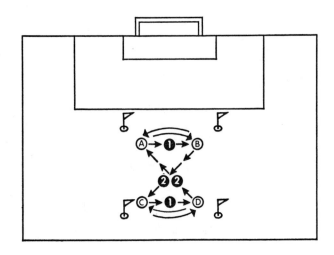

Drill 7–4

Square—Diagonal—Exchange Positions

Drill 7–4   Square—Diagonal—Exchange Positions

No. of players   4 per drill group.

Equipment   4 flags or cones to mark off a 10-yard square.

Explanation   On a whistle signal A passes to B and C passes to D. The passes should be on the ground. Then B and D pass diagonally across the square. At this point, A and B change places, and C and D exchange places. D sprints to receive B's diagonal pass, and B sprints to receive D's diagonal pass.

Order of passes   Square—diagonal.

Purpose   Players practice exchanging positions. Players practice controlling and passing a ball.

Drill 7–5   Three-on-Three Plus One (No Diagram)

No. of players   7 per drill group.

Equipment   4 flags or cones to mark off the 15-yard square.

Explanation   This is a game of three-on-three keep-away with an extra player on the side who has possession of the ball. Each time a team loses possession of the ball, the extra player joins the team that possesses the ball.

Purpose   Players learn to adjust to numerical superiority. Players practice trapping, passing, and tackling in a confined area.

Drill 7–6   Pass and Exchange

No. of players   3 per drill group.

Equipment   4 flags or cones to mark off the 10- to 15-yard square.

Explanation   A passes to player B. After passing, A exchanges places with player C, and so on. Each time a pass is made, the player making the pass exchanges positions with the player not involved in the pass. A different player receives the ball each time it is passed. (The diagram shows three phases of the drill in the same grid.)

Purpose   Players practice exchanging positions and movement off the ball. This technique is used to confuse the opposing team.

Drill 7–7   Double Grid—One-on-One

No. of players   3 per drill group.

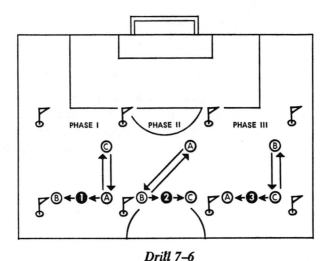

Drill 7–6

Pass and Exchange

Equipment 6 cones or flags to mark off two 10-yard grids.

Explanation The defense players set up at the far end of each grid. When player A enters the first grid, a defensive player enters grid one and tries to clear the ball out of the grid. If A beats the defensive player in grid one, he continues to grid two and is challenged by the second defensive player. A's objective is to dribble through both grids.

Purpose Players practice dribbling, feinting, and tackling skills in a confined area.

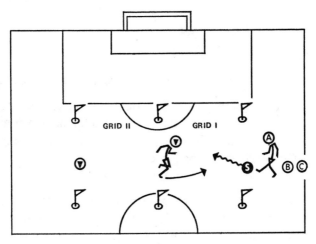

Drill 7–7

Double Grid—1 on 1

Chapter Eight

Relating Moving Passing Drills to Match Play

Discipline, concentration, and patience are necessary in order to maintain and control a ball until an opportunity develops for a shot on the goal. These attributes can be learned by practicing the following drills and exercises. In these drills, a small group of players learns progressive passing and supporting patterns.

Overlapping, decoying, and other tactical elements are an important part of the moving passing drills. Through participation in and practice of these drills, players develop a tactical awareness that will carry over to a game situation.

It is important that these drills be introduced after players become proficient at passing and receiving skills. Otherwise, frustration and confusion will develop if they cannot pass accurately and trap a ball quickly. It would be like "putting the cart before the horse." In general, introduce these drills at a point where the players have a good chance to successfully carry out the requirements of each drill.

Each player should be aware of what his movements will be in relationship to those of the ball. Key words referring to the movement of the ball, such as "through," "square," "diagonal," and "back" will help players think ahead and, in turn, will add efficiency and continuity to the drill. Once these drills have been mastered, further variations can be introduced. For instance, have two groups perform moving passing patterns at either end of the field. As they pass through each other around mid-field, the players must concentrate on the task at hand in order to successfully pass through the other drill group. In doing so, they learn the need for discipline in pass execution.

Another variation is the addition of defenders to the drill. Place defenders at the far end of the field. The prescribed pattern of passing and receiving continues until the attacking drill group reaches the immediate area of the defenders at the far end of the field. At this point, the drill group is permitted to break out of its set pattern and attempt to beat the defenders with any pattern or maneuver that will better their chances of getting a shot at the goal.

In early attempts at this variation, you should give the numerical superiority to the attacking group. For example, start with three attackers against one defender—three-on-one. Finally, attempt the drill with an even number of attackers and defenders.

In general, moving pass drills enable a team to acquire the discipline and the ability to concentrate in small groups, which are necessary for team play. Through practice of these prescribed patterns of play, players are better prepared to cope with the varied challenges they will be confronted with in match play.

Drill 8–1   Two-Man Pass and Loop

No. of players   2 per drill group.

Distance   A to B—5 to 10 yards.

Explanation   All passes are straight ahead. A passes to B. A overlaps and takes up a new position in front of B. B passes to A, B overlaps and takes up a new position in front of A, and so on.

Purpose   Players practice passing and overlapping while moving the ball down the field.

Drill 8–2   Triangle—Reformation

No. of players   3 per drill group.

Distance   A, B, and C form a triangle. A to C—5 to 10 yards, C to B—5 to 10 yards, A to B—5 to 10 yards.

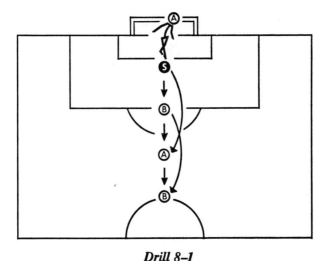

Drill 8–1

2 Man Pass and Loop

Explanation A passes to C, A runs between C and B to reform the triangle. The player in control of the ball may sometimes be required to delay a pass until the triangle is reformed.

Purpose Players practice moving the ball up the field while forming and reforming a triangle.

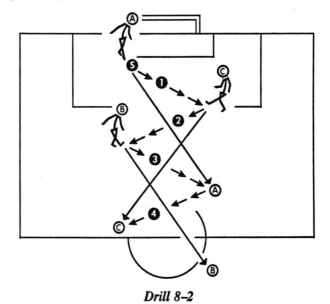

Drill 8–2

Triangle—Reformation

Drill 8–3   Give and Go Down the Field

No. of players   5 per drill group.

Distance   A to B—5 to 10 yards, B to C—5 to 10 yards, etc.

Explanation   A passes diagonally to player B. B sends a square pass back to A. A repeats the same procedure with players C, D, and E. When A reaches the last player, E, he kicks the ball back to player B, who moves over to become the active player. A gets in line with D, C, and E. This drill is resumed, with B as the active moving player.

Purpose   Players practice multiple give-and-go passes.

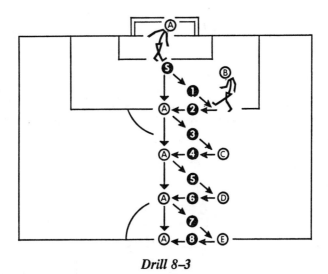

Drill 8–3

Give and Go Down the Field

Drill 8–4   Zigzag

No. of players   12—6 per drill group.

Distance   See the diagram for the position of the players involved.

Explanation   A and B are fullbacks, C is a halfback, D is a wing, and E is a forward. The drill is started by the goalkeeper (G) rolling the ball to player A. A passes to B. B passes to C. C passes to D. D crosses the ball over the field to E. E takes a shot at the goal. This same procedure occurs on the other side of the field.

Purpose   Players practice a pattern for moving the ball up the field. At the same time, they are practicing passing, trapping, and shooting.

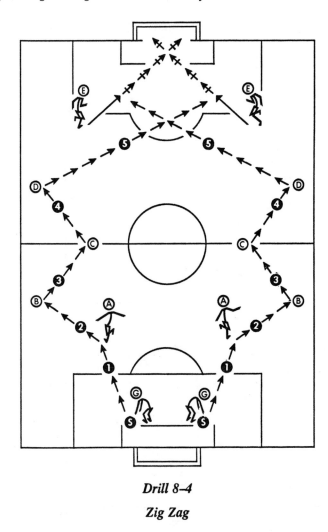

Drill 8–4

Zig Zag

Drill 8–5   Team Chipping

No. of players   2 per drill group.

Distance   A to B—30 to 40 yards.

Explanation   Player A chips across the field to player B. B dribbles a few yards and passes (chips) back to A. This procedure is repeated down the field until A or B passes off to A or B at the other end of the field. The same procedure is repeated up the field by this other group.

Purpose   Players practice long chip passes needed in a game situation.

These passes are used to change the attack from one side of the field to the other.

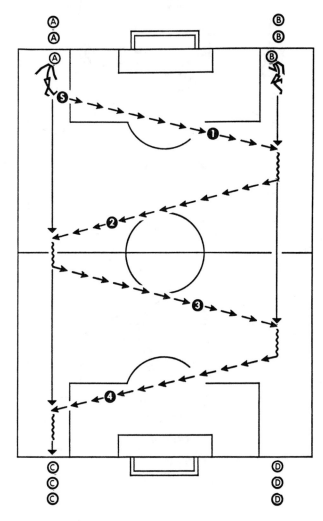

Drill 8–5

Team Chipping

Drill 8–6   Two Man Square Lead Pass

No. of players   2 per drill group.

Distance   A to B—5 to 10 yards.

Explanation A square passes to B. B pushes the ball straight ahead. A runs diagonally to receive B's lead pass. A then square passes to B, and B pushes the ball straight ahead, and A runs diagonally to receive the lead pass. This procedure is repeated down the field. B passes straight ahead, and A square passes. Both A and B run diagonally after passing the ball.

Purpose Players practice moving the ball down the field by lead and square passes.

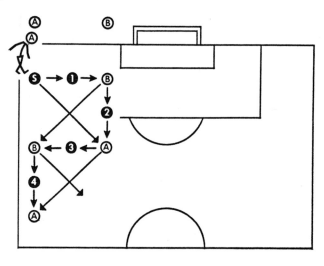

Drill 8–6

2 Man Square—Lead Pass

Drill 8–7 Square Passing

No. of players 5 per drill group.

Distance A to B—10 to 15 yards, B to C—10 to 15 yards, etc.

Explanation A passes across to B, B passes ahead to C. C sends a square pass to A. A returns the pass back to C. C passes ahead to D, and so on. Each time A returns the pass, he moves down the field and repeats this procedure with the next player in line.

Purpose Players practice moving the ball down the field in a set pattern.

Drill 8–8 Random Moving Passing (No Diagram)

No. of players 2 per drill group.

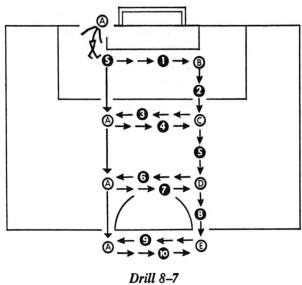

Drill 8–7

Square Passing

Distance   A to B—4 to 5 yards apart.

Explanation   A passes to B when B calls for the ball. Both players move down the field, and B should move in a random fashion. One time he runs and circles A and calls for the ball; the next time he runs to A's right and calls for the ball. It is up to A to make a good pass to B no matter where B moves to.

Purpose   Player A learns to adjust his pass according to the position of player B.

Drill 8–9   Two-Man Pass—Back Pass—Dribble—Pass Off

No. of players   2 per drill group.

Distance   A to B—4 to 5 yards apart.

Explanation   A passes forward to B, B passes back to A. A dribbles until he is adjacent to B and then passes off to B. A then runs 5 yards ahead of B, and the drill is repeated as the players move down the field.

Purpose   Players practice a two-man combination pass used to move the ball down the field.

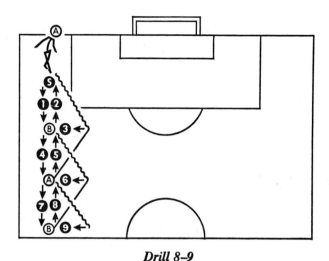

Drill 8–9

2 Man Pass, Back Pass, Dribble, Pass Off

Drill 8–10   Two-Man Pass—Sprint—Dribble

No. of players   2 per drill group.

Distance   A to B—15 to 20 yards.

Explanation   A passes diagonally to player B. A sprints behind B, while B dribbles to the other side and passes back to A who has taken up a

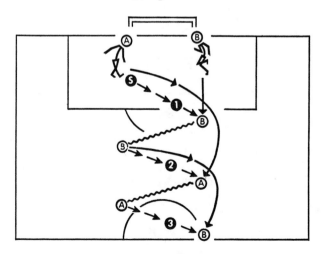

Drill 8–10

2 Man Pass, Sprint, Dribble

position on the other side. This procedure is continued down the field.

Purpose   Players practice passing and exchanging positions while moving down the field.

Drill 8–11   Two-Man Push Forward and Overlap

No. of players   2 per drill group.

Distance   A to B—15 to 20 yards.

Explanation   A passes diagonally to player B. B taps the ball forward a few yards and sprints off to the other side. A sprints around and behind B to pick up the ball. A passes diagonally across to B, who taps the ball forward. The drill is continued down the field.

Purpose   Players practice moving the ball down the field while overlapping and exchanging positions.

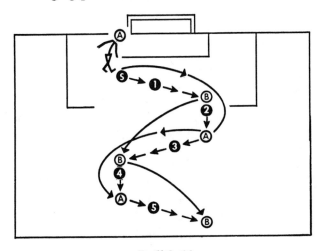

Drill 8–11

2 Man Push Forward and Overlap

Drill 8–12   Two-Man Crisscross Pattern

No. of players   2 per drill group.

Distance   A to B—10 to 20 yards apart.

Explanation   A lead passes to B. B collects the ball and dribbles diagonally forward while A crosses diagonally behind B. Ball exchanges are made diagonally forward and into the space between the two players.

Purpose Players practice a basic crisscross pattern while moving down the field.

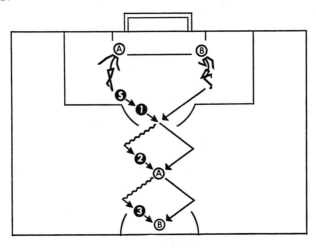

Drill 8–12

2 Man Criss-Cross Pattern

Drill 8–13   Dutch Passing Running Drill I (lead, square, back)

No. of players 3 per drill group.

Distance A to B—10 yards, B to C—10 yards.

Explanation A dribbles a few times and sends a lead pass to B. B dribbles a few times and sends a square pass to C. C then back passes to A and this cycle is repeated down the field. First attempts at this drill should be at a slow pace. Each player must learn when to delay in order to maintain a good position from which to receive the next pass.

Purpose Players practice moving the ball down the field using lead, square, and back passes.

Drill 8–14   Dutch Passing Running Drill II (lead, square)

No. of players 3 per drill group.

Distance A to B—10 yards, B to C—10 yards.

Explanation A sends a lead pass to B. B dribbles a few times and sends a square pass back to A. A then dribbles a few times and sends a lead pass to C. C dribbles a few times and sends a square pass back to player A. This routine is repeated down the field.

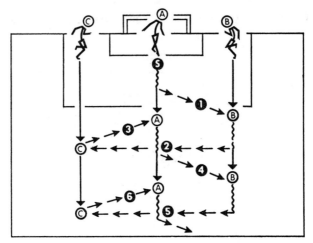

Reprinted with permission from Soccer World
1400 Stierlin Road, Mountain View CA 94043

Drill 8–13

Dutch Passing Running Drill I—Lead, Square, Back

Purpose   Players practice moving the ball down the field, using lead and square passes.

Drill 8–15   Dutch Passing Running Drill III (lead passes)

No. of players   3 per drill group.

Distance   A to B—10 yards, B to C—10 yards.

Explanation   A lead passes to B. B dribbles a few times and sends a lead pass to C. C dribbles a few times and sends a lead pass back to B. This routine is continued down the field.

Purpose   Players practice moving the ball down the field using lead passes.

Drill 8–16   Dutch Passing Running Drill IV (lead, square, back)

No. of players   9 (3 groups of 3 players)

Distance   A to B—10 yards, B to C—10 yards.

Explanation   A of group I dribbles a few times and sends a lead pass to B. B dribbles a few times and sends a square pass to C. C then back passes to A. This cycle is repeated down the field. When players from group I get to the end of the field, they pass to A in group II, and group II

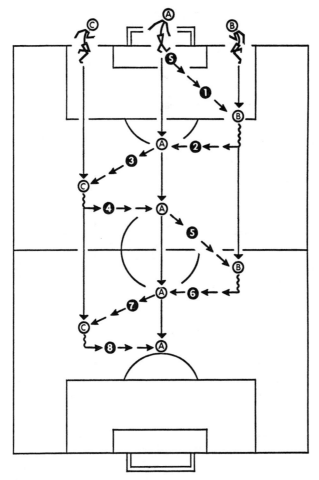

Reprinted with permission from Soccer World
1400 Stierlin Road, Mountain View CA 94043

Drill 8–14

Dutch Passing Running Drill II—Lead, Square

performs the same drill going up the field. This same procedure is re-peated with group III. Play is continuous.

Purpose Players practice moving the ball down the field using lead, square, and back passes.

Drill 8–17 Dutch Passing Running Drill V (lead, square)

No. of players 12 (4 groups of 3 players)

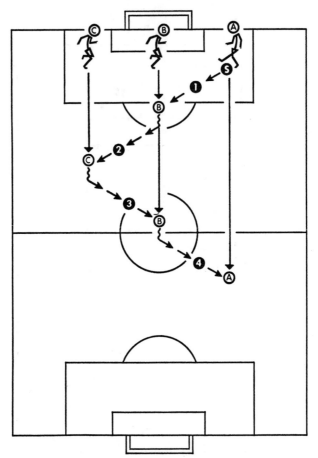

Drill 8–15

Dutch Passing Running Drill III—Lead Passes

Distance   A to B—10 yards, A to C—10 yards.

Explanation   Group I and group II start up the field at the same time, while group III and group IV wait their turn. This drill is performed in the same manner as Dutch Passing Running Drill I, except that the two teams start at the same time and pass through each other in the middle of the field. Special concentration is necessary in performing this drill. After groups I and II complete the drill, groups III and IV start the same maneuvers.

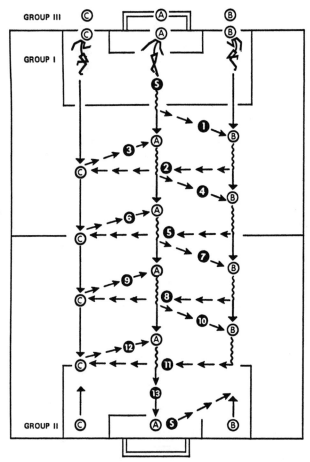

Reprinted with permission from Soccer World
1400 Stierlin Road, Mountain View CA 94043

Drill 8–16

Dutch Passing Running Drill IV—Lead, Square, Back

Purpose   Players learn to perform and concentrate under pressure from another group of players moving in the opposite direction.

Drill 8–18   Pass Through and Overlap

No. of players   9—3 groups of 3 players

Distance   A to B—10 yards, A to C—10 yards.

Explanation   Play starts with player A in group I. A passes ahead to player B. A then overlaps B. B passes to C; B overlaps C, and so on.

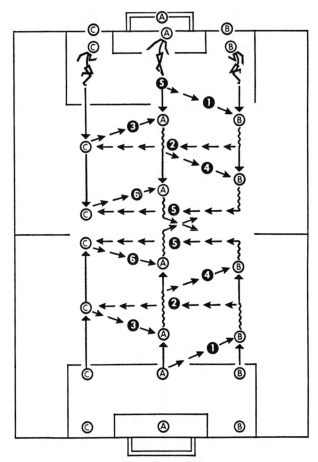

Drill 8–17

Dutch Passing Running Drill V—Lead, Square

When the first group of players reaches the other end of the field, they pass off to group II. Group II repeats the drill up the field and passes off to group III. The player passing the ball should make sure that his pass is well ahead of the intended receiver.

Purpose Players practice passing and overlapping at a high rate of speed.

Drill 8–19   Middleman

No. of players   3 per drill group.

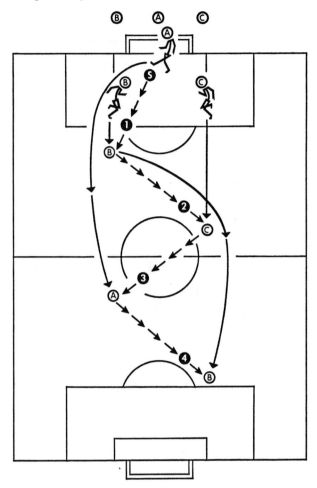

Reprinted with permission from Soccer World
1400 Stierlin Road, Mountain View CA 94043

Drill 8–18

Pass Through and Overlap

Distance A to B—10 yards, B to C—10 yards.

Explanation Starting with A, the ball is passed to the middleman, player B. The ball is always passed to the middleman by the outside players A and C.

Purpose Players practice moving the ball down the field.

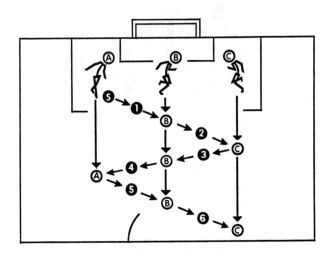

Drill 8–19

Middle Man

Chapter Nine

Relating Small-Group Passing Drills to Match Play

An attacking team has two general responsibilities: First, to distribute players systematically so that they can control the largest area possible without becoming too spread out. This is known as having depth, width, and balance in your attack. Second, the players should support and concentrate in the area of the ball; that is, create and use to their advantage their numerical superiority. This chapter concerns this second area of responsibility.

Through the years, certain tactical maneuvers that increase a team's chances of using space to its advantage, for instance, the use of a wall pass in a two-on-one situation, have been identified and developed. In this chapter you will find many small-group tactical maneuvers used for advancing a ball in situations that occur frequently in a game. The drills teach players to handle these situations automatically and quickly. Each drill in this chapter incorporates one or more of the following deceptive or diversionary tactics that create opportunities and penetrate the defense:

Wall Passes: Force defenders to play the ball and to open space for a penetrating pass.

Back Passes: Create space and draw defenders out of position.

Crisscross Runs: Force defenders to decide which player to follow or to guard.

Decoy Runs: Draw defenders away from an area of the field.

Diagonal Runs: Make the defense line up and draw defenders from an area of the field.

Loop Runs: Make the defense think you are going in a certain direction, after which you quickly loop back and reverse the direction.

Exchanging Positions: Enables players to maintain width and depth for supporting each other. Also confuses the defense.

Quick Switching and Blind Side Runs: Surprise the defense.

Return Passing: Draws the defense toward the ball so they will open space.

Each of these diversionary tactics should cause your opponents to react in a predictable manner. If they do not, players should be prepared with alternative methods of meeting the challenge. For example, when executing a wall pass, a player dribbles toward a defender to commit him; the defender backs off and guards the player's teammate. Through practice, players will learn to react quickly to the new situation by keeping the ball and dribbling off.

Once your players can perform these drills, you should provide them with competitive game-like experiences in small groups. Start with a small group of players; as skill improves, increase the number of players in each group until you have a full-team scrimmage. During these games, you should encourage players to use the small-group passing maneuvers that they have learned in the drilling process.

The following order of progression can be used to develop and to give game-like experiences in the use of small-group passing maneuvers:

2 on 1	4 on 2	5 on 3	6 on 4	7 on 6
2 on 2	4 on 3	5 on 4	6 on 5	7 on 7, etc.
3 on 1	4 on 4	5 on 5	6 on 6	
3 on 2				
3 on 3				

As the group becomes larger, increase the playing area. In a 2-on-1 game, use a 10-yard square, in a 5-on-5 game, use half of the field; and in a game of 8-on-8, use the entire field.

To increase the versatility of your players, you can add certain variations to these small-sided games. Each of these play variations emphasizes different facets of the game that would never be practiced unless special attention was called to them. To vary the games:

1. Limit players to 1 and 2 touches of the ball.
2. Play with no goals, with 2 goals, or with 4 goals.
3. Limit the area of play; use the full field.
4. Play a game where only passes on the ground are permitted.
5. Play a game where players can only use their weak foot in passing the ball.

Sometimes a combination of two or more of these variations can be used in a game. In using these play variations, keep in mind that the main purpose of these small-sided games is to practice small-group passing maneuvers.

The ability of a small group of players to execute these drills quickly and with assurance will increase the chances of a team penetrating another team's defense.

Drill 9–1   Wall Pass and Shoot

No. of players   2 per drill group.

Distance   B to A—10 to 15 yards.

Explanation   A passes to B. B returns the pass. A shoots at the goal on a "one-touch" shot. A takes B's place, and B gets behind A's line.

Purpose   Players practice wall passing and "one-touch" shooting.

Drill 9–2   Double-Wall Pass

No. of players   3 per drill group.

Distance   A to B—5 to 7 yards, B to C—5 to 7 yards.

Explanation   Player A passes to player B, B passes back to A. A passes

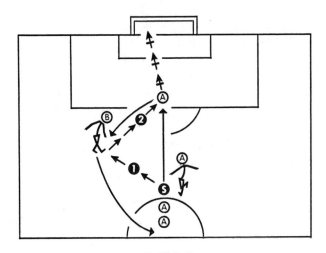

Drill 9–1

Wall Pass and Shoot

to C, and A receives a pass back from C. A takes a shot at the goal.

Purpose Players practice double-wall passing.

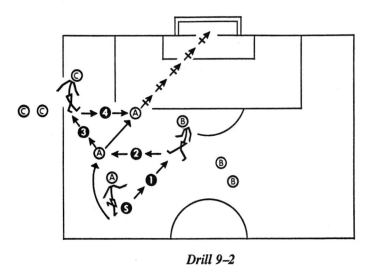

Drill 9–2

Double Wall Pass

Drill 9–3 Through the Legs

No. of players 3 per drill group.

Distance A to C—10 to 15 yards, A to B—5 to 10 yards.

Explanation A passes to B. B lets the ball pass between his legs. B turns and passes off to C, who takes a shot at the goal.

Purpose Players practice going with the ball when it is passed to them.

Variation B lets the ball go to either of his sides and runs with it before he passes off.

Variation B opens his legs and deflects the ball of his heel to player C.

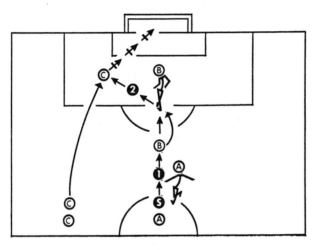

Drill 9–3

Through the Legs

Drill 9–4 Right Mid-Field Cross

No. of players 3 per drill group.

Distance A to B—5 to 10 yards, B to C—5 to 10 yards.

Explanation A passes to B, and B returns the pass. C breaks to the outside to receive a pass from A. B makes a decoy run to the open space ahead of him. In team play, A is a fullback, B is a halfback, and C is a wing.

Purpose Players practice penetrating the defensive territory by using a decoy run.

Variation Practice the same drill on the other side of the field.

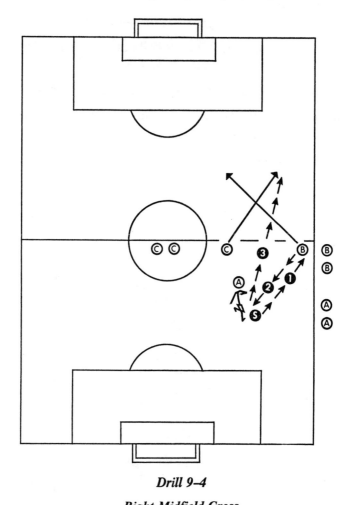

Drill 9–4

Right Midfield Cross

Drill 9–5 Mid-Field Setup for a Crisscross

No. of players 3 per drill group.

Distance A to C—20 to 30 yards. B stands in the penalty arc area.

Explanation At mid-field, A dribbles across the field and passes off to C. A continues across the field and veers toward the 18-yard line. At this point A receives a pass from C. A then passes into player B who has come forward to receive the pass. A and C then crisscross in front of player B. B passes off to A or C, depending upon which player is clear for a shot on goal.

Purpose   Players practice a crisscross pattern and use diagonal running in order to penetrate the defense. The secondary purpose of this drill is to practice trapping, passing, and shooting.

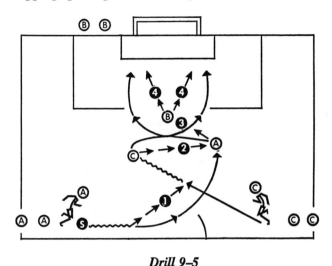

Drill 9–5

Midfield Set-up for a Criss-Cross

Drill 9–6   Mid-Field Setup for a Straight Run

No. of players   3 per drill group.

Distance   A to C—20 to 30 yards; B stands on the penalty arc area.

Explanation   At mid-field, A dribbles across the field and passes off to player C. A continues across the field and cuts toward the 18-yard line. A, who is moving toward the 18-yard line, receives a pass from C. A then passes to B, who moves forward to receive the pass. A and C then sprint straight down the field to receive a pass from B. B passes to whichever player is open to receive a pass. A and C represent halfbacks, and B represents a forward.

Purpose   The primary purpose of this drill is for players A and C to make diagonal runs in order to confuse the defense. The secondary purpose is to practice trapping, passing, and shooting drills.

Drill 9–7   Dribble, Back Pass, and Decoy

No. of players   3 per drill group.

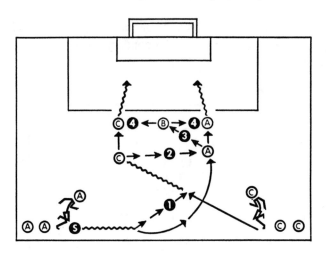

Drill 9–6

Midfield Set-up for a Straight Run

Distance   B to C—10 to 12 yards, B to A—5 to 7 yards.

Explanation   A dribbles into the corner and back passes to B. C makes a decoy run to draw the defense. A runs to the space previously occupied by C. B passes to A. A shoots at the goal.

Purpose   Players practice creating open space by using a decoy run to free a player for a penetrating pass.

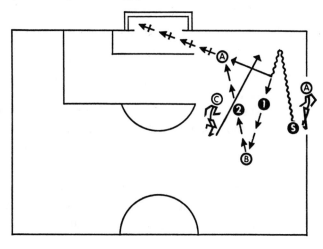

Drill 9–7

Dribble, Back Pass and Decoy

Drill 9–8   Long Pass and Decoy

No. of players   3 per drill group.

Distance   G to B—35 to 40 yards, B to A—20 to 30 yards.

Explanation   A makes a decoy run and B fills the space made available by A's decoy run.

Purpose   Player A practices a decoy run to provide an area for a long pass to player B.

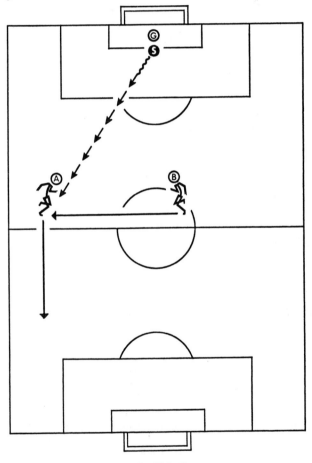

Drill 9–8

Long Pass and Decoy

Drill 9–9   Back Pass and Stay

No. of players   3 per drill group.

Distance   A to B—5 to 10 yards, C to B—5 to 7 yards.

Explanation   A passes forward to B, B passes back to C. C returns the pass to B. C breaks toward the goal to receive a pass. C takes a shot at the goal.

Purpose   This is a simple back passing combination used to confuse the defenders.

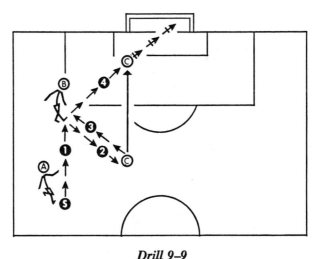

Drill 9–9

Back Pass and Stay

Drill 9–10   Diagonal and Reverse Run

No. of players   6 per drill group.

Distance   B to C—5 yards, B to A—5 yards.

Explanation   B and C make diagonal runs to the left and then cut toward the right side of the field. Player B receives a pass from player A. A should pass the ball early to prevent B and C from being caught offsides.

Purpose   Players practice making diagonal and cut-back runs in order to penetrate the defense.

Drill 9–11   Step on It

No. of players   3 per drill group.

Distance   A to B—10 to 15 yards.

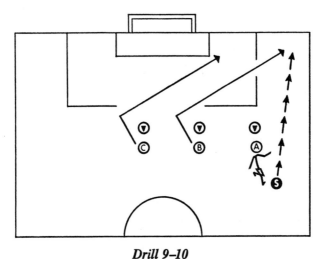

Drill 9–10

Diagonal and Reverse Run

Explanation A dribbles diagonally towaid the defensive player. Just before he reaches the defensive player, A leaves the ball behind him, B picks it up and continues dribbling.

Purpose This drill is practiced as a basic passing pattern when two players are running down the field side by side and encounter a defensive player. It is one way of dealing with a two-on-one situation.

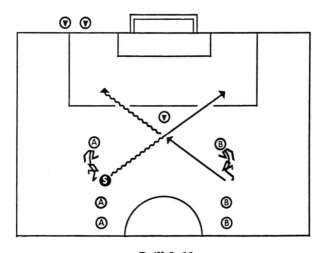

Drill 9–11

Step On It

Drill 9–12   Cross-Decoy

No. of players   4 per drill group.

Distance   A to B—7 to 10 yards, A to C—5 to 7 yards.

Explanation   A passes off to B. C makes a decoy run. B dribbles straight ahead and passes back to A. A takes a shot at the goal.

Purpose   Players practice making a decoy run and a crossing pattern in order to penetrate the defense.

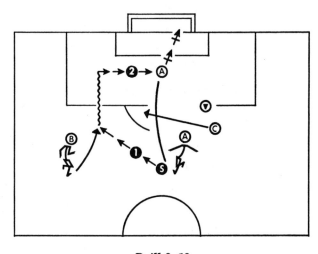

Drill 9–12

Cross Decoy

Drill 9–13   Diagonal Decoy and Dribble

No. of players   2 per drill group.

Distance   A to B—10 to 15 yards.

Explanation   A passes diagonally forward to B. B dribbles diagonally toward the corner of the 18-yard line. A runs behind B and then runs straight down the field to receive a return pass. A takes a shot at the goal.

Purpose   This play used to penetrate the defense. B creates open space by dribbling diagonally to draw the defender away from player A.

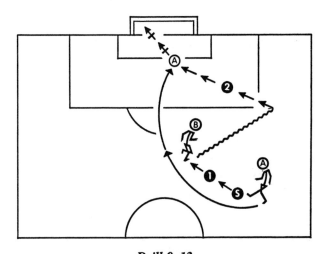

Drill 9–13

Diagonal Decoy and Dribble

Drill 9–14 Opposite Side

No. of players 2 per drill group.

Distance A to B—10 to 15 yards.

Explanation A passes back to player B. B waits for A to move to the right or to the left. B passes to whichever side A moves to, then runs to the opposite side. B receives a return pass and shoots at the goal.

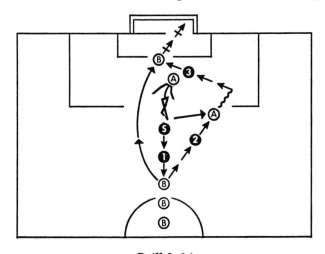

Drill 9–14

Opposite Side

Purpose   Players practice a simple drill used to penetrate the defense. A creates open space and draws defenders away from player B.

Drill 9–15   Back Pass and Go

No. of players   3 per drill group.

Distance   A to B—15 yards.

Explanation   Player A passes to player B. B quickly returns the pass to player A. B runs across the field to receive a return pass from A. B gathers the ball and takes a shot at the goal.

Purpose   This is a simple drill to be used when offensive players find themselves lined up one ahead of the other, and facing each other. The defensive players are drawn out so that they can be vulnerable for penetration by the offense.

Player A will learn that if he receives a quick return pass from player B, player B will break for the goal in an attempt to get clear for a return pass. This drill is used in conjunction with the overlap drill.

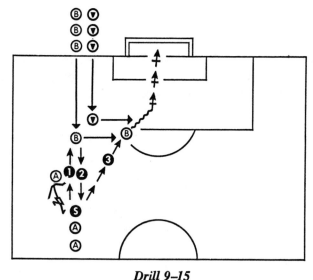

Drill 9–15

Back Pass and Go

Drill 9–16   Overlap

No. of players   3 per drill group.

Distance   A to B—15 yards.

Explanation Player A passes to player B who runs out to receive the pass. If player B hesitates and does not pass immediately back to A, player A should run toward the goal, at an angle away from player B, to receive a return pass. A then takes a shot at the goal.

Purpose This is a simple drill for players who find themselves lined up one ahead of the other. It draws the defense out and enables the offensive players an opportunity to penetrate. Players also learn to meet the ball instead of standing back and waiting for it to come to them.

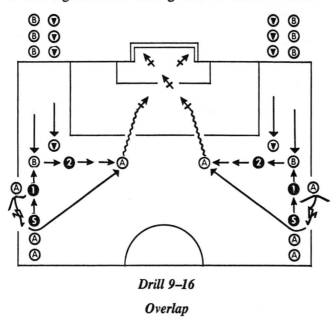

Drill 9–16

Overlap

Drill 9–17   Two-on-One Commit and Pass Off

No. of players   3 per drill group.

Distance   A to B—4 yards, A to the defensive player—15 yards.

Explanation Player A dribbles directly toward the defensive player. Once A has committed the defensive player, he passes off to player B. The drill is ended by player B taking a shot at the goal. Players A and B rotate positions. Defensive players get into the back of their lines.

Purpose This is a simple drill to be used when offensive players find themselves lined up one beside the other. This drill is designed to make the defensive players commit themselves so that the offense can penetrate.

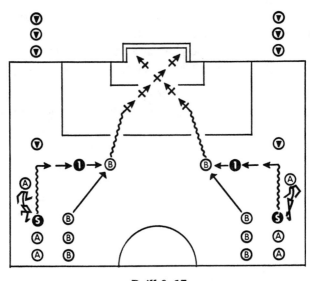

Drill 9–17

2 On 1 Commit and Pass Off

Drill 9–18   Scissors

No. of players   3 per drill group.

Distance   A to B—10 to 15 yards apart, A and B to the defensive player—15 to 20 yards.

Explanation   Player B runs in front of and across the face of the defensive player, and is followed immediately by Player A dribbling the ball. If the defensive player follows player B, player A dribbles in for a shot at the goal. If the defensive player does not follow player B and hesitates, player A passes off to player B, who takes a shot at the goal.

Purpose   This is a simple drill used when offensive players find themselves lined up one beside the other. The defensive player must decide whether to follow player A or player B. Whichever is the case, one of the two offensive players will be free to take a shot at the goal.

Drill 9–19   Loop Back Decoy

No. of players   3 per drill group.

Distance   A to B—10 yards, defensive player to B—1 yard.

Explanation   B runs laterally and quickly cuts back to receive a pass from A. B takes a shot at the goal.

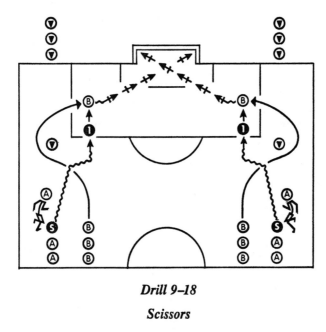

Drill 9–18

Scissors

Purpose B creates open space by first moving across the field, then quickly looping back.

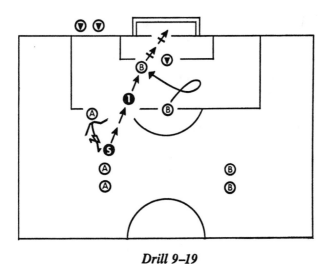

Drill 9–19

Loop Back Decoy

Drill 9–20 Overlap Draw

No. of players 3 per drill group.

Distance   A to B—7 to 10 yards, B to the defensive player—3 to 5 yards.

Explanation   A passes to and overlaps B. B then returns the pass to A. B makes a run behind the defensive player to receive a chip pass from A, and B takes a shot at the goal.

Purpose   The two-man overlap is used to draw the defense in one direction and to pass back to the other direction.

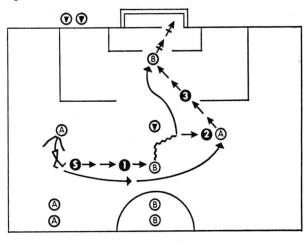

Drill 9–20

Overlap Draw

Drill 9–21   Three on Two Decoy

No. of players   5 per drill group.

Distance   A to C—10 yards, A to B—10 yards, defensive players are 4 yards away from C and B.

Explanation   A passes off to B, and A makes a decoy run to attract the defensive player toward the middle of the field. B passes back to the space created by A's decoy run. C receives the pass and continues dribbling down the field for a shot at the goal.

Purpose   Players practice a decoy run to advance the ball down the field.

Drill 9–22   Fake Overlap

No. of players   3 per drill group.

Distance   A to B—5 to 10 yards, B to the defensive player—1 to 3 yards.

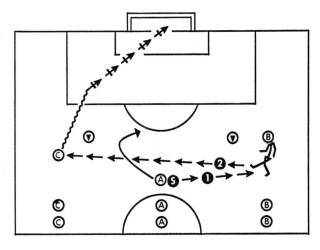

Drill 9-21

3 on 2 Decoy

Explanation A passes to B, then overlaps B to receive a return pass. B makes a decoy run to draw the defense out of the play. A dribbles to the 18-yard line and takes a shot at the goal.

Purpose This is a play used in conjunction with the overlap draw play. When the defense becomes familiar with the overlap draw, this play is used to deceive the defense. (See drill 9-20 for the overlap draw drill.)

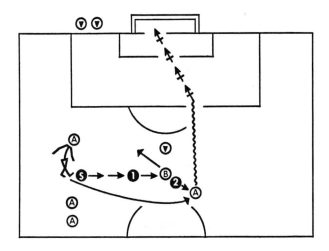

Drill 9-22

Fake Overlap

Drill 9–23   Fake Draw

No. of players   3 per drill group.

Distance   A to B—7 to 10 yards, B to the defensive player—1 to 2 yards.

Explanation   Player A passes to player B, B fakes a return pass to A, who has overlapped player B. B dribbles to the left of the defensive player to the 18-yard line, where he shoots at the goal.

Purpose   This play is used in conjunction with the overlap draw play and the fake overlap play. The difference in this play is that player B doesn't pass back to player A.

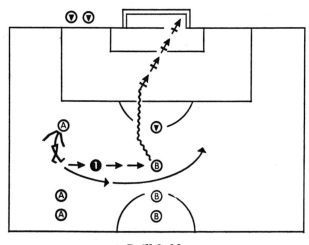

Drill 9–23

Fake Draw

Drill 9–24   Heel Drill

No. of players   3 per drill group.

Distance   A to B—10 to 15 yards.

Explanation   A dribbles across and in front of the defensive player. At the same time B crosses behind A and receives a heel pass or a sole-of-the-foot back pass. B takes a shot at the goal. Timing is important in this drill.

Purpose   Players practice back heel passing and sole-of-the-foot back passing. Players practice maneuver that will help them create an opportunity for a shot on goal.

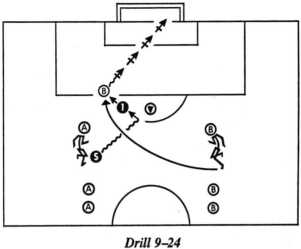

Drill 9–24

Heel Drill

Drill 9–25   Switching and Decoy

No. of players   3 per drill group.

Distance   B to C—40 yards, A to B—30 yards.

Explanation   A passes diagonally to B, A then runs in front of B and makes a loop run to delay his run at the goal for a shot. B dribbles behind A and square passes to C who is running forward to meet the pass. C then passes to A, and A takes a shot at the goal.

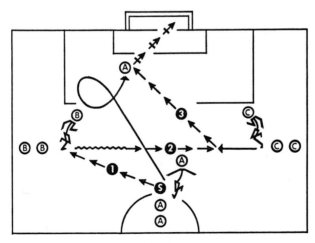

Drill 9–25

Switching and Decoy

Purpose Players practice decoy and delayed runs to develop proper timing. Players also practice switching the player from one side of the field to the other.

Drill 9–26   V-Decoy Run

No. of players 6 or more to each drill group.

Distance A to B—20 to 25 yards.

Explanation A passes back to B. B dribbles a few times to give A enough time to make his decoy run, as shown in the diagram. B passes to A, and A shoots at the goal. Players then change lines.

Purpose Players practice a basic decoy run pattern.

Variation Add a defensive player behind player A.

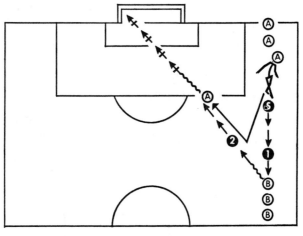

Drill 9–26

V-Decoy Run

Drill 9–27   Post Man

No. of players 6 or more per drill group.

Equipment A supply of soccer balls.

Explanation A passes to C, A and B cross in front of C. The defensive player is to mark either A or B, depending upon which player is unguarded. A or B shoots at the goal.

Purpose Player C receives practice at making quick decisions and passing to the open man.

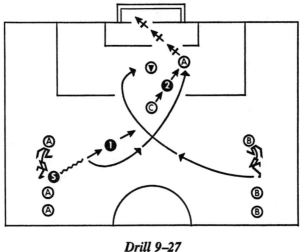

Drill 9–27

Postman

Drill 9–28 Quick Switching

No. of players 3 per drill group.

Distance A to B—5 to 7 yards, A to C—25 to 35 yards.

Explanation A dribbles toward the right corner. A steps on the ball and runs to the corner. B immediately crosses the ball to C who takes a shot at the goal.

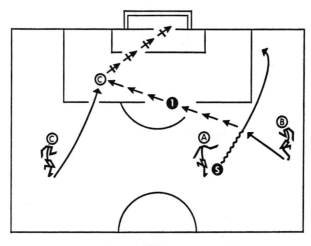

Drill 9–28

Quick Switching

Purpose   This is a basic drill for quickly switching the direction of the play to the other side of the field.

Drill 9–29   Parallel Leave It

No. of players   3 per drill group.

Distance   A to B—10 to 15 yards.

Explanation   Player A dribbles across and toward player B, and in front of the defensive player. As players A and B cross, player B picks the ball up and dribbles it around the defensive player. B then passes back to player A.

Purpose   Players practice switching the direction of the flow of play in an attempt to confuse the defense.

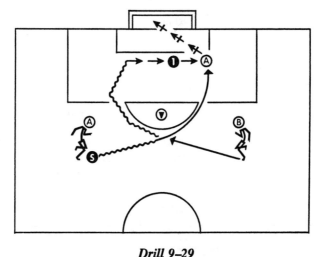

Drill 9–29

Parallel Leave It

Drill 9–30   Decoy Combination

No. of players   4 per drill group.

Distance   A to C—15 to 20 yards. A to D—5 to 7 yards, D to B—5 to 7 yards.

Explanation   B makes a decoy run and receives a pass from A. B immediately passes off to C. D moves into the space created by B's decoy run. C passes to D.

Purpose This is a basic pattern used to create open space by a decoy run.

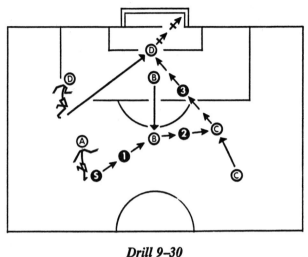

Drill 9–30

Decoy Combination

Drill 9–31 Back Pass Diversion

No. of players 3 per drill group.

Distance B to A—15 to 20 yards.

Explanation A passes to B as B runs toward A. The defensive player attempts to cover B, who returns the pass to A. B then runs around the group of players that are waiting their turn to take part in the drill, and receives a pass from A. B dribbles toward the 18-yard line and attempts a shot on goal.

Purpose Players develop speed and endurance in a two-on-one situation.

Drill 9–32 From Behind and Wall Pass

No. of players 4 per drill group.

Distance B to the point of reception—5 to 7 yards, C to B at the time of B's reception—5 to 7 yards.

Explanation C is a forward and a stationary player. A passes the ball to B. B collects the ball, and passes on the ground to C. C returns the pass,

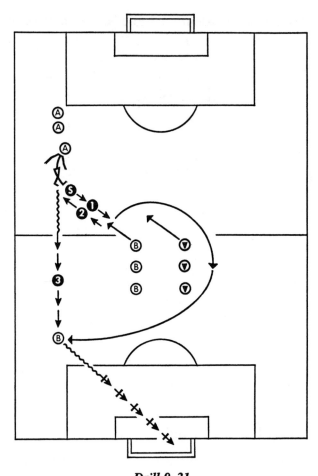

Drill 9–31

Back Pass Diversion

and B shoots at the goal. B takes A's place, and A goes to the end of B's line.

Purpose This drill is practice for halfbacks and fullbacks to come through from their positions in the rear to a shooting position.

Drill 9–33 Cross Pass and Shoot

No. of players 3 per drill group.

Distance A to C—10 to 12 yards, C to B—10 to 12 yards.

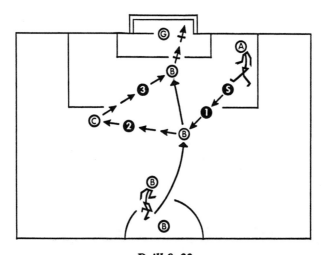

Drill 9–32

From Behind and Wall Pass

Explanation A passes across to B, who passes to C. C shoots at the goal, and must delay and time his run.

Purpose Players practice passing, trapping, shooting, and switching the ball to the other side of the field.

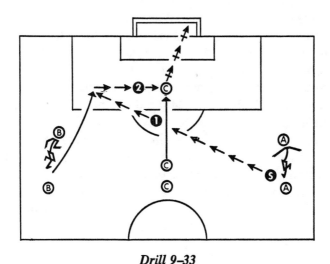

Drill 9–33

Cross Pass and Shoot

Section Three

Special Situations

Soccer is a game of continuous play. Absolute set plays are rarely used during this continuous play, although at times, the game is sometimes interrupted because the ball goes out of bounds or over the end line, or because a referee stops play when a rule has been broken. These situations are not part of the normal play of continuous action, and are therefore called special situations. When play is resumed, a set play is used by the attacking team. It is an established fact that many goals are scored during the executing of these special situations. Therefore, you should prepare your players to be able to take advantage of them.

These special situations are effective in scoring many goals because the play is temporarily stopped. During this time, the attacking team is able to take up positions which tactically improve their chances of scoring. Further, the kicker is not under pressure. In every special situation, with the exception of the throw-in, the opposing team is required to be ten yards away from the player restarting the action. As a result of this lack of pressure on the person restarting the action, greater accuracy in the placement of the ball occurs, and in turn, scoring opportunities are more likely to occur.

In each of the special situations, there are various tactics that are commonly used: decoy runs, cross over runs, change of pace runs, diagonal runs, and other diversionary tactics are used to divert the opponents' concentration. After leading your opponents in one direction, you quickly turn and go in another one.

How special situations are handled depends upon the ability and talent of your players. You need to identify special talents such as good headers, accurate shooters, long throwers, long kickers, and so forth. Afterwards, you can determine the proper use of these talents and then you devise set plays to fit the abilities of your players. Finally, constant practice to improve the timing and execution of play is necessary so that these maneuvers become habitual and precise.

Life is like a special situation: it doesn't always work out the way we plan it. In any case, we should be prepared to improvise, so that an alternate plan can be used. This same axiom holds true for special situation plays. Even though you plan for the situation to be handled in an automatic fashion, your players should be provided with alternate methods of handling the situations.

Chapter Ten

Relating Corner Crossing and Corner Kicks to Match Play

Tactically, corner kicks and corner crossing are similiar in that in both cases the ball approaches the goal from the same area. For this reason, corner crossing drills and corner kicking drills have been placed in the same chapter.

Certain special situations occur over and over again in a soccer game. One of these situations is corner crossing. It occurs frequently because defense systems permit much more activity out near the touch-lines than they do in front of the goal or in the middle of the field.

At this point, you may ask, What is the difference between a corner kick and a corner crossing? In a corner kick, the play is temporarily stopped. During this time, players are able to take positions that tactically improve their chances of scoring; the kicker can take his time and deliver the ball without pressure. There are no offsides, and players can get closer to the goal to receive the ball.

In corner crossing, the tactics are similar, yet different; the defensive pressure is continuous: the kicker is being marked, and other attacking players must observe the offsides rule. In this situation there is more pressure, therefore, passes are not as accurate. Further, the element of surprise cannot be used to a greater advantage than a play started with distractions.

In match play, many goals are scored from the corner area. As a result, emphasis and time should be placed on preparing players to attack corners of the playing field. This will enable them to take maximum advantage of the situation when it occurs in a game.

When a ball is approaching or is already in the corner area, other attackers should be prepared to move into the goal area. The timing of these runs is most important.

There are two methods for arranging attacking players to meet the ball in a corner kick situation: they are stationing players and echelon formation. In both methods, the basic idea is to distribute players so that they cover the entire goal area. In the stationed method, players are stationed inside the goal area and move about to cause congestion and confusion. Sometimes decoy runs are made to provide open space, establishing a target area for the kicker. Then a player from outside the goal area moves into the open space to take a shot on the goal. In the echelon formation, four or five players outside the goal area move into it as a unit, and should arrive just as the ball arrives.

Whether the echelon system or the stationed system is used, players should position themselves so that they can head or kick the ball on the run. Players on the run can jump higher; consequently, they have a better chance to head the ball into the goal.

The question arises, At what spot on the field should the kicker aim the ball? For the most part, this depends upon the position of the defending players. But in general, it should be kicked just outside the far side of the goal area. It should also be kicked far enough so that it will be dangerous for the goalkeeper to come out after it. Most coaches agree that the ball should be an out swinger. In other words, the arc of the flight of the ball should curve toward the attacking players.

Short corner kicks are sometimes used to draw defenders out of the goal area. When the defenders are drawn out, the ball is kicked behind them, and another player moves into the area from the rear to kick it at the goal.

In defending against corner kicks, the goalkeeper should stand near the far third of the goal post. One defender should guard the far post, and one defender the near post. Another defender should be in position, in front of the goal area nearest the kicker, to prevent low crosses across the goal mouth. In this way, all players are able to see the approaching ball. All other defensive players should assume man-for-man coverage.

The kicker has three options in corner crossing patterns: one, to chip the ball high to the far post; two, to drive the ball to the near post for a quick deflection; and three, to dribble along the base line and pass the ball back diagonally toward the penalty area so a player from the rear can advance and kick it into the goal. Where the defenders stand determines which option the kicker chooses. Certain drills in this chapter provide practice for deciding which option to choose: the far post, the near post, or passing back.

In defending against a corner crossing, the goalkeeper moves toward the near post to cut down the angle of a possible shot. Other players are tending to their zone or guarding an opponent, depending upon the defense system the team is using. The different defenses against a corner kick and a corner crossing arise from the fact that in a corner crossing play, the offsides rule is in effect. Also, there is a definite need at this time for the attacking team to maintain its width to keep the defense spread out. In a corner kick, play is temporarily suspended during the corner kick, and the attacking players have time to organize in and throughout the immediate area of the goal.

Drill 10–1   Two-on-One Wing Cross

No. of players   3 per drill group.

Distance   A to B—5 to 10 yards, A to the defensive player—5 to 7 yards.

Explanation   B makes a run for the corner while A pushes a pass to the open space in the corner. A then breaks toward the goal to receive a crossed ball from B. A shoots at the goal. B should be a mid-fielder, and A should be a wing forward.

Purpose   This drill is used to practice setting up a scoring opportunity by players exchanging positions.

Drill 10–2   Straight Wing Cross with a Delayed Run

No. of players   2 per drill group.

Distance   A to B—15 to 20 yards.

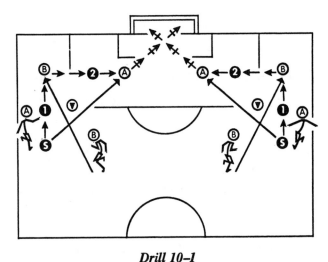

Drill 10–1

2 On 1 Wing Cross

Explanation A dribbles down the touchline and deep into the corner area to cross his ball. B makes a diagonal run to receive the cross from player A, then shoots at the goal. B is a striker and A is a wing forward.

Purpose This drill is used to practice a straight wing cross attack. Player B practices timing his run so that he will meet the pass from player A on the run.

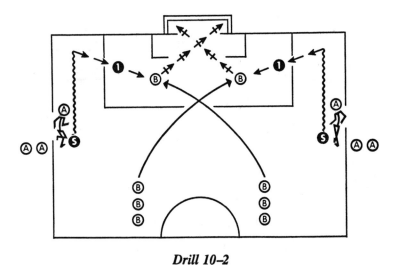

Drill 10–2

Straight Wing Cross with a Delayed Run

Drill 10–3   Wing Attack and Recovery

No. of players   7 per drill group.

Distance   A to C—20 to 30 yards, A to B—20 to 30 yards.

Explanation   A passes across to player B. B dribbles down the field and toward the defender. Player B should try to pull the defender toward the middle of the field. Just as B comes near to the defender, B turns and sprints down the sideline. If B can beat the defender, he crosses the ball and the attack continues. If at any time the ball is lost, A, B, and C must sprint back over the half-field mark before a defender can dribble the ball over the mark. Once the offense loses the ball, they do not try to recover it. They get back to the half-field line as quickly as possible.

Purpose   Players practice wing attack play and at the same time become aware of defensive responsibilities after they lose the ball.

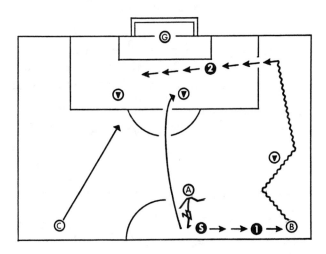

Drill 10–3

Wing Attack and Recovery

Drill 10–4   Reverse Passing

No. of players   3 per drill group.

Distance   A to B—1 yard, B to C—1 yard.

Explanation   B starts the drill by making a short run toward the right touchline. B cuts back to receive a pass from A. B kicks a long high kick to the edge of the left side of the penalty area. A runs for the near post and

B runs for the far post. C gathers B's pass and immediately crosses the ball to the far post. If the pass is short, A heads the ball into the goal.

Purpose   Players practice deceiving opponents into thinking the ball is going to the right side of the field, when the play is actually to the left side of the field.

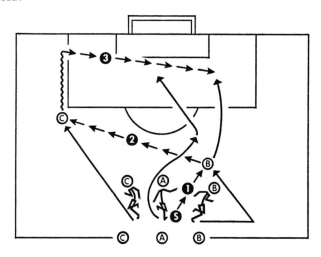

Drill 10–4

Reverse Passing

Drill 10–5   Corner Timing

No. of players   2 per drill group.

Distance   A to B—5 to 10 yards.

Explanation   A passes to B. B sprints to the corner and gives the signal "GO." This is a signal for player A to start sprinting so that he can meet the crossed ball on the run.

Purpose   This drill develops timing in meeting crossed balls.

Drill 10–6   Crisscross Blind Side Run

No. of players   3 per drill group.

Distance   A to B—15 to 20 yards, B to C—15 to 20 yards.

Explanation   A dribbles a few times, and then passes straight ahead to the open space. B races to meet the pass, then crosses to C who takes a

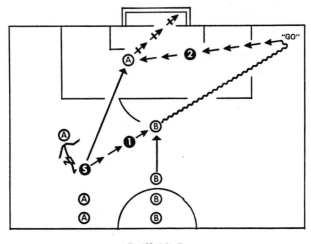

Drill 10–5

Corner Timing

shot at the goal. In the event that the ball is poorly kicked and B's pass does not reach player C, player A then rushes in to shoot the ball.

Purpose   Players practice switching the ball from one side of the field to the other.

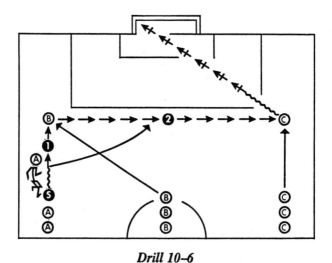

Drill 10–6

Criss-Cross Blind Side Run

Drill 10–7   Cross Over Cross

No. of players   3 per drill group.

Distance   A to B—15 to 20 yards.

Explanation   A dribbles to his right and passes diagonally to player B. In the meantime, C makes long run behind A, and C receives a pass from B. C dribbles to the corner area and crosses the ball to A or B.

Purpose   Player C changes positions and overlaps to exploit the defense.

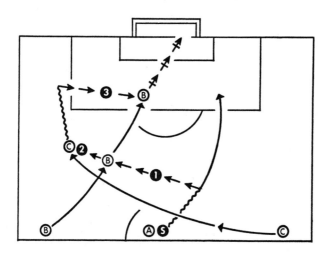

Drill 10–7

Cross Over Cross

Drill 10–8   Decoy and Cross

No. of players   7 per drill group.

Distance   A to B—10 to 15 yards, A to C—5 yards, A to D—5 to 10 yards.

Explanation   C and D make a decoy run to draw the defensive player to the left side of the field. A square passes to player B, B dribbles down the touchline to the corner and crosses the ball in front of the goal.

Purpose   This drill is used to draw the defense to the other side of the field in order to get into position to cross the ball in front of the goal.

Drill 10–9   Overlap and Decoy

No. of players   5 per drill group.

Distance   A to C—5 yards, A to B—5 yards.

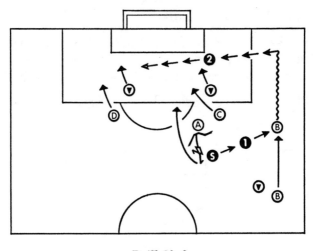

Drill 10–8

Decoy and Cross

Explanation   A square passes to B. C overlaps and receives a pass from B. C dribbles to the corner area and crosses the ball to B or A. The two defenders guard A and B.

Purpose   This drill uses a decoy and an overlap maneuver to get the ball deep into the corner for a cross.

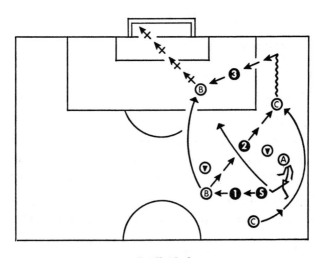

Drill 10–9

Overlap and Decoy

Drill 10–10   Wing Crisscross

No. of players   6 per drill group.

Distance   A to B—10 to 15 yards, A to C—10 to 15 yards.

Explanation   A dribbles toward the corner. The outside players or wings crisscross at the 18-yard restraining arc. B receives a pass from A and B takes a shot at the goal.

Purpose   In this drill, players practice a crisscross pattern in order to confuse the defense.

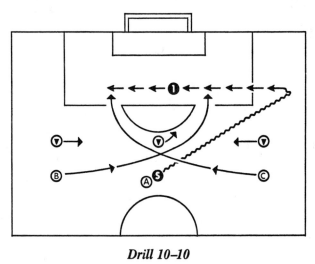

Drill 10–10

Wing Criss Cross

Drill 10–11   Switching Sides

No. of players   7 per drill group.

Distance   A to B—5 to 7 yards, B to D—15 to 20 yards, D to C—5 yards.

Explanation   A dribbles toward the defender who is in front of him. When the defender moves to mark A, he passes back to B. B immediately passes to the space in front of C, who takes a shot at the goal. D makes a decoy run. The 3 defenders guard A, B, and D.

Purpose   Players practice switching the play to the other side of the field.

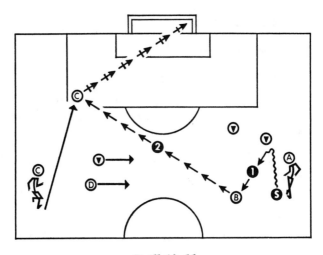

Drill 10–11

Switching Sides

Drill 10–12   Corner Kick Draw

No. of players   2 per drill group.

Distance   A to the defender—1 to 2 yards.

Explanation   A tries to deflect the ball off the defender's leg. The objective is to make the ball go out of bounds after it hits the defender's legs.

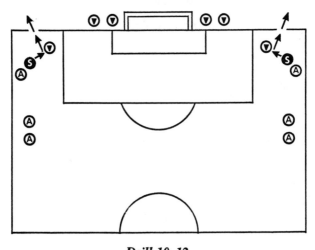

Drill 10–12

Corner Kick Draw

Purpose   Players practice this technique to be used when an offensive player gets into trouble close to the end line. It is a technique used to draw corner kicks.

Caution   No wild kicking.

Drill 10–13   Cross and Shoot

No. of players   4 per drill group.

Distance   A to B—20 to 30 yards.

Explanation   The goalkeeper throws the ball to player A. A chips the ball to B. B dribbles down the touchline and crosses the ball. C takes a shot at the goal.

Purpose   Players practice crossing and shooting the ball at the goal.

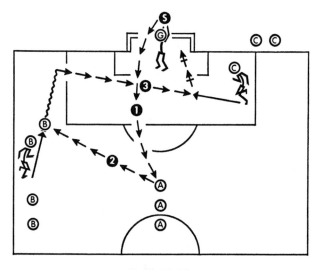

Drill 10–13

Cross and Shoot

Drill 10–14   Corner Kick Drill I

No. of players   5 per drill group.

Distance   A to B—20 to 30 yards.

Explanation   B runs toward the corner yelling for the ball. B then slows down and yells "NO" to deceive the defense. B then curves his run and receives a pass from A, then he dribbles along the end line till he can make a back pass to player C. C shoots at the goal. To avoid being caught offside, A steps back out of bounds.

Purpose   In this drill B makes a fake run in order to get behind the defense.

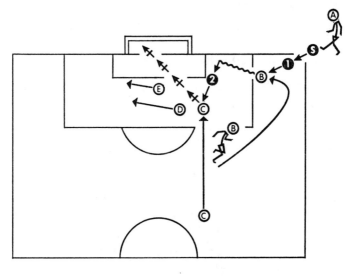

Drill 10–14

Corner Kick Drill I

Drill 10–15   Corner Kick Drill II

No. of players   6 per drill group.

Distance   A to B—20 to 30 yards.

Explanation   C starts the play by making a run toward A yelling or calling for the ball. C stops inside the goal area as seen in the diagram. Player B runs toward the corner. A kicks the ball to player B, who immediately crosses the ball to the far post.

Purpose   The defense is drawn to one side of the field, then the ball is crossed to the other side of the field.

Drill 10–16   Corner Kick Drill III

No. of players   6 per drill group.

Distance   A to C—40 to 50 yards.

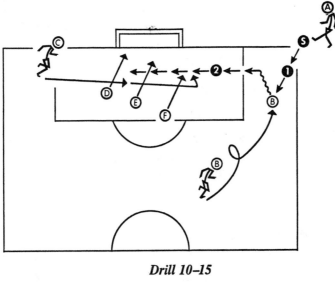

Drill 10–15

Corner Kick Drill II

Explanation   B runs from the other side of the field to receive a short pass from player A. B deflects the ball to player C, who takes a shot at the goal. C circles back in order to confuse the defense.

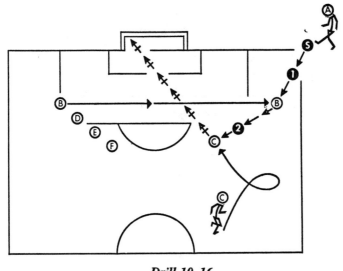

Drill 10–16

Corner Kick Drill III

Purpose   The offensive team uses a short corner kick to create an opportunity for a shot at the goal by player B's long run across the field.

Drill 10–17   Corner Kick Drill IV

No. of players   5 per drill group.

Distance   A to C—30 to 40 yards.

Explanation   Players C and D make a decoy run. As C and D make their run, A kicks the ball to the space in front of player B. B runs to the ball and shoots at the goal. All other players line up on the left side of the field.

Purpose   Players C and D make a decoy run to create a scoring opportunity for player B.

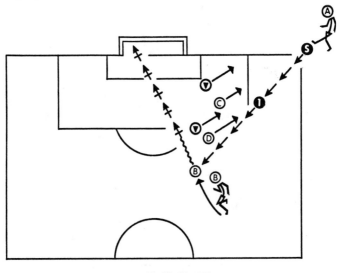

Drill 10–17

Corner Kick Drill IV

Chapter Eleven

Relating Throw-In Drills to Match Play

Strategy in a throw-in situation depends upon where the throw-in takes place. If the throw-in is intercepted at the extreme ends of the field, the situation can be critical. If the throw-in is intercepted in the middle of the field, it is not as critical. In any case, the defenders, as well as the attackers, must adjust their positions quickly because a fast throw-in is frequently used to catch defensive players napping.

The throw should be taken quickly, should achieve maximum penetration, and, at the same time, it should assure that possession is maintained. All receiving players should be on the move. The following tactical maneuvers are used to free players from defenders: exchanging positions; crisscross runs; decoy runs; exploiting weaknesses such as throwing to players guarded by short opponents; change-of-pace runs, and veer runs which entail running in one direction, then quickly changing the run to another direction.

The thrower should conceal where he intends to throw the ball. He does this by faking a throw down the field, then quickly turning and throwing to the other end of the field. He can fake a short throw and deliver a long throw; he can fake to one player and throw to another.

A strategy frequently used when all receiving players are tightly marked is heading or passing the ball back to the thrower. This procedure is logical because the thrower is rarely marked. Another strategy is to overload a section or an area near the thrower. Then, when possession of the ball is attained, players spread out in order to reestablish attacking width.

A throw-in, taken in the attacking area of the field, can sometimes result in a goal. This is especially true when a member of your team can throw long distances. A long throw into the area near the goal, and a quick deflection sometimes ends up in the goal. Also, since the offsides rule is not in effect during throw-in plays, players are able to get closer to the goal to take advantage of this situation.

If you use four fullbacks in defense, throw-ins can be taken by the wing fullback. In this way, the wing forwards, other forwards, and mid-field players are able to move into positions that will produce greater penetration.

Throw-ins taken near the middle of the field are not as critical, because neither the threat of being scored upon nor the opportunity to score are immediate possibilities. Maintaining possession of the ball is the key objective.

In throw-ins taken in the defending area by the attacking team, use a wing forward or a mid-field player. This will enable the defensive player to concentrate on defense if the ball is intercepted. Frequently, a throw-in deep in the defending area is thrown to the goalkeeper, who then starts the attack. The goalkeeper can get greater distance on the throw, and the ball is less likely to be intercepted.

In defending against a throw-in near your own goal, defenders should not mark the thrower in order to be able to use the extra player as a sweeper to stop a breakthrough, if it develops. Close marking is recommended, and all players should be on the alert because the offsides rule is not in effect.

Throughout the game, the throw-in is sometimes used as a long term weapon against the opponents, that is, if your team is in superior physical condition. Quick throw-ins cause the opponents to be constantly on the move. Therefore, the opponents become exhausted, especially during the later stages of the game. To further exhaust your opponents, you can speed up the way you take goal kicks and free kicks.

Drill 11–1   Throw-In to the Goalkeeper

No. of players   3 per drill group.

Distance   Refer to the diagram.

Explanation   On a signal, the goalkeeper (G) and the defensive player race to receive the ball thrown by player A. For this drill, the goalkeeper stands on the goal line in the middle of the goal. The defensive player stands on the other side of the penalty-area restraining arc line. This line-up will give a slight advantage to the goalkeeper.

Purpose   In many instances, the goalkeeper can start an attack more effectively than the thrower. This drill gives the goalkeeper practice in catching a ball while under pressure from an opposing player.

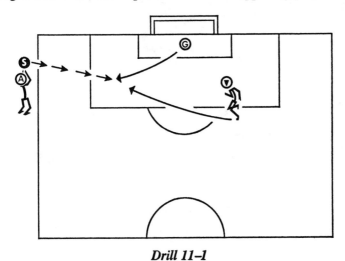

Drill 11–1

Throw In to the Goalkeeper

Drill 11–2   Tall Man Throw-In

No. of players   5 per drill group.

Distance   A to B—18 to 20 yards, A to C—15 to 20 yards.

Explanation   B is the tallest man on the team. A throws high to B, who runs toward A to receive the throw-in. B heads the ball to C just inside the 18-yard line. C then shoots at the goal.

Purpose   This drill is designed to score a goal from a throw-in by utilizing the physical attributes of player B, who is the tallest man or the best jumper on the team.

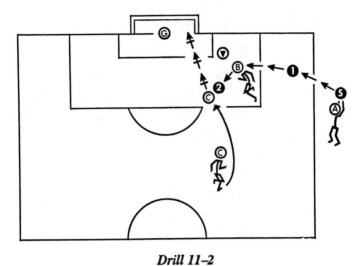

Drill 11–2

Tall Man Throw In

Drill 11-3 Throw-In Pressure

No. of players 3 per drill group.

Distance A to the defense player—10 to 20 yards.

Explanation A throws the ball into the space in front of B. B runs to the

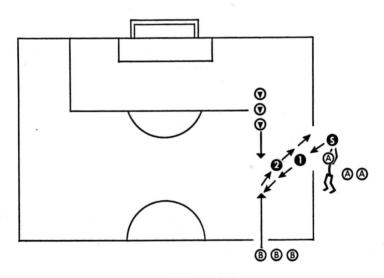

Drill 11–3

Throw In Pressure

ball and immediately heads or passes back to A. The throw should be timed so that B gets to the ball just before the defender arrives.

Purpose   Players practice throwing the ball in-bounds in a pressure situation.

Drill 11–4   Head Return

No. of players   2 per drill group.

Distance   A to B—20 to 30 yards.

Explanation   A throws to B, then steps into the field of play. B heads back to A, and goes to the end of the line. B should head the ball down to the ground when returning the ball to player A.

Purpose   Usually the defensive team will not guard the player who is throwing the ball. For this reason the thrower is free to receive a return pass. It is a well-known fact that player B is at a disadvantage because he is facing away from the goal, whereas the thrower (A), is facing the attacking goal. For this reason, practicing this drill is important in developing a sound offensive attack from a throw-in.

Variation   Add a defender behind player B.

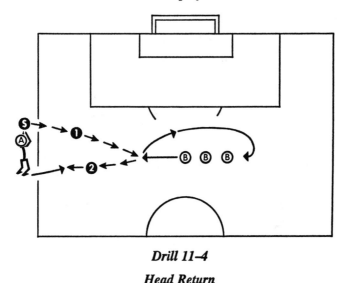

Drill 11–4

Head Return

Drill 11–5   Crisscross Throw-In

No. of players   5 per drill group.

Distance   C to B—20 to 30 yards.

Explanation   Players C and B make a crisscross run. A throws to whoever is clear to receive the throw-in.

Purpose   In this drill, crisscross runs are made to confuse the defensive players.

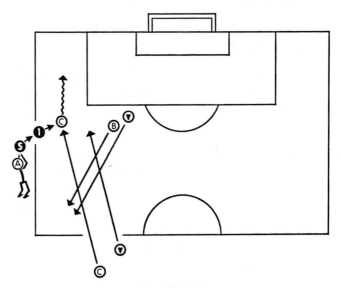

Drill 11–5

Criss Cross Throw In

Drill 11–6   Give and Go Throw-In with a Decoy

No. of players   5 per drill group.

Distance   A to where B receives the throw-in:—10 yards, C to B—3 to 5 yards.

Explanation   B runs forward to receive the throw-in from player A. B heads or kicks the ball back to A, who is running toward the middle of the field. Player C makes a decoy run to draw defenders away from player A.

Purpose   Players practice getting the ball in-bounds by using a return pass and a decoy run.

Drill 11–7   Veer Run

No. of players   3 per drill group.

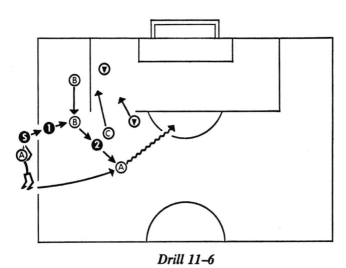

Drill 11–6

Give and Go Throw In with a Decoy

Distance A to B—15 to 20 yards.

Explanation Player B loses his defender by making a run back toward the thrower and pulling his defender with him. As player B approaches player A, he veers and sprints down the touchline to receive the throw-in.

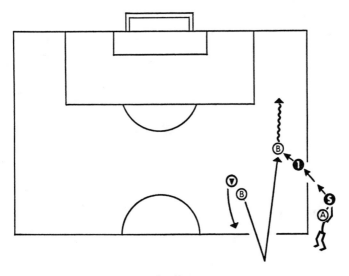

Drill 11–7

Veer Run

Purpose   Players practice this maneuver to break a player free to receive a throw-in.

Drill 11–8   Multi-Purpose Throw-In

Distance   Refer to the diagram.

Explanation   B runs down the field to receive the throw-in from player A, then heads the ball to C's feet. B continues his run down the touchline to receive a return pass from player C. B dribbles to the corner area and crosses the ball to player D, who shoots at the goal.

Purpose   Players practice a wall pass immediately after receiving a ball from a throw-in. Players practice the following techniques: throwing, heading, crossing, trapping, and shooting.

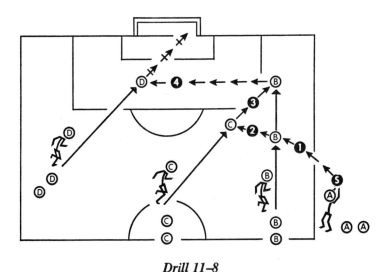

Drill 11–8

Multi Purpose Throw In

Drill 11–9   Down the Line

No. of players   2 per drill group.

Distance   A to B—20 to 30 yards.

Explanation   B makes a run straight down the field and cuts toward the touchline. A sends a lead pass to B, then comes on the field and follows the play. A receives a pass from player B, and dribbles toward the penalty area to either shoot or to pass off to another player.

Purpose Players practice a play to confuse the defense and to advance the ball into the penalty area.

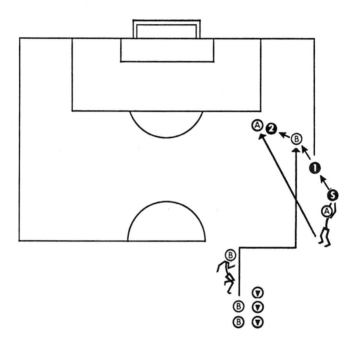

Drill 11–9

Down the Line

Drill 11–10 "J" Throw-In

No. of players 2 per drill group.

Distance A to B—25 to 35 yards.

Explanation Player B runs back in the defending area to receive the throw-in from player A. A makes a diagonal run to receive a return pass.

Purpose Players practice a give-and-go throw-in play to move the ball down the field toward the goal.

Drill 11–11 Loop Run

No. of players 5 per drill group.

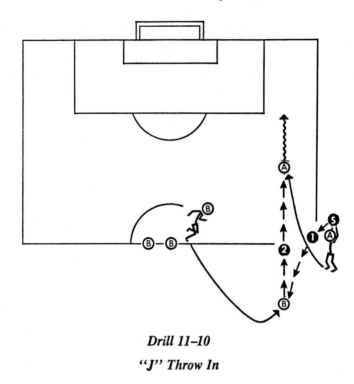

Drill 11–10

"J" Throw In

Distance A to B—5 to 10 yards, B to C—5 to 7 yards.

Explanation B makes a decoy run to make way for player C to receive the throw-in from player A. C dribbles into the corner area and crosses to player B, who shoots at the goal. B times his loop run in order to meet the ball on the run.

Purpose Players practice this drill to increase their opportunities of scoring a goal by utilizing decoy and loop-back runs to get behind the defending players.

Drill 11–12   Throw-In

No. of players   5 per drill group.

Distance   A to B and C—15 to 20 yards.

Explanation   C runs behind B's defensive player in order to free himself to receive the throw-in from player A.

Purpose   This is a simple procedure used to evade a defender in order to receive the throw-in.

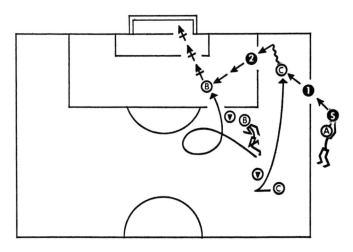

Drill 11–11

Loop Run

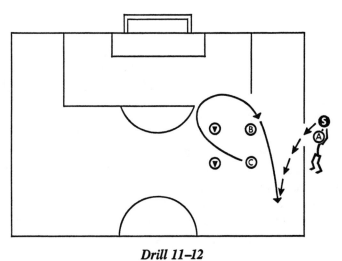

Drill 11–12

Throw In

Chapter Twelve

Relating Free Kicks and Goal Kicking to Match Play

When a free kick is awarded and a shot at the goal is not a good possibility, the kick should be taken as quickly as possible to catch the defense napping. For this reason, all players should be ready to take the free kick when it occurs in their immediate area. But when the free kick is awarded within shooting range and a shot at the goal looks promising, it should be taken by the player on the team with the best kicking ability. This player should have an accurate, powerful shot, and he should be able to curve the ball around the wall. In the section on passing, you will find a drill for practicing ball curving.

When the free kick is awarded within shooting range of the goal, the defense will set up a wall to shut off access to the near side of the goal. In most cases, 4 or 5 players are sufficient to accomplish this. The goalkeeper covers the far side of the goal. In this case, the attacking team has the choice of going around the wall, over it, or trying to blast through it. Sometimes in the early stages of the game, the kicker will blast the ball at the wall to unnerve the defenders. This will cause defenders to flinch and to make unproductive movements. Also, this procedure may be productive later in the game when other free kicks are awarded.

If the wall is not properly set up, the kicker should seriously consider shooting at the goal. Otherwise, some type of deceptive maneuver to go over, around, or through the wall is used.

In going through the wall, a player sometimes will fake the kick and step over the ball in order to make the individual forming the wall move out of position. Then a teammate comes from behind to blast the ball at the goal.

A second method to beat a wall is to fake a blast at the wall and step over the ball. A teammate then pushes the ball out to the side of the wall, and another player comes up from the rear and shoots at the goal.

Attempting to chip the ball over the wall requires accuracy and timing. Players should be on the run, yet they should be cautious to remain onsides.

No matter what method is used to exploit this free-kick situation, the attackers should keep the defense guessing about what will happen. Surprise will work miracles in this situation.

In defending against free kicks within shooting range, players would set up a wall as quickly as possible. If the kick is awarded off to the side of the goal, the goalkeeper should arrange the players in the wall to cover the far post. The goalkeeper and the other defense players should position themselves so they can see the ball. If the kick is awarded directly in front of the goal, a split wall is sometimes used, and the goalkeeper stands in the middle of the goal so that he can see the ball as it is kicked.

Immediately after the ball is touched, the members of the wall should move out as a unit toward the ball to cut down the angle of possibility of further action. After the ball is won and is under control, the defending team should quickly reestablish itself to get ready for an attack.

When the goalkeeper moves out after the ball, another player should be assigned to cover the goal for him during his absence.

Preparing to meet the challenges of free kick situations requires much time and repetitive practice, but it is worth the effort because the rewards are great. Many goals are scored from a free kick situation.

In the free kick category, special attention is needed for preparing players to take goal kicks. Maintaining possession of the ball is the first consideration when attempting a goal kick. The kicker should remember that a poor kick could cause a quick goal to be scored for the opponents.

Before kicking, the kicker should survey the situation and decide whether or not to get the ball off quickly. He should decide whether the element of surprise will be to the advantage of the team.

Next the kicker should pick out the farthest unmarked player down the field and consider the possibility of kicking the ball to him. Frequently, a player out near the touchlines is loosely marked and is the logical choice for the kick.

Finally, if all players down the field are closely marked, the kicker should consider passing the ball outside the penalty area to a fullback. The fullback can then return the pass to the goalkeeper, if it is not safe for him to make progress up the field. In this way, the goalkeeper can start the attack by throwing the ball long or short with his hand, depending upon what the situation dictates.

Throughout the entire goal-kicking procedure, all attacking players should be ready to funnel back into their defensive positions if the ball is intercepted.

Drill 12–1   Free Kick Drill I.

No. of players   10 per drill group.

Explanation   D stands as if he is going to take the kick. Instead, A pushes the ball to the right to player B. A continues his run, yelling for a return pass, but B kicks the ball out to C, and C shoots at the goal. C comes from behind, pretending that he is not involved in the play.

Purpose   This is a play used to get the ball around a wall by pretending it is going in one direction, and then quickly passing it to the other direction.

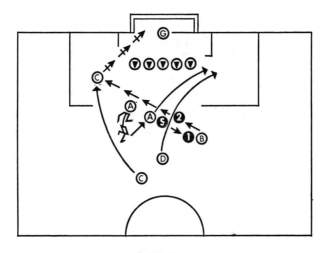

Drill 12–1

Free Kick Drill I

Drill 12–2   Free Kick Drill II.

No. of players   8 per drill group.

Explanation   B and C cross in front of the defensive wall. A has three options: over the wall, around the right side of the wall to C, and around the left side of the wall to player B.

Purpose   This drill gives practice at beating a defensive wall by going around or over it.

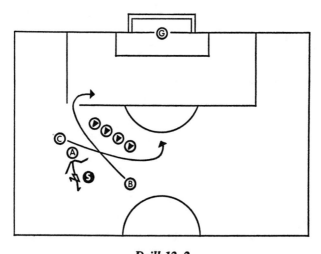

Drill 12–2

Free Kick Drill II

Drill 12–3   Free Kick Drill III.

No. of players   11 per drill group.

Explanation   A passes to B. D makes a decoy run to draw defenders away from the play. B passes to C. C turns and shoots at the goal. All other players decoy away from the play.

Purpose   This drill is practice for beating a defensive wall by going around it. Decoy runs are used to create an opening for the play to proceed into.

Drill 12–4   Free Kick Drill IV.

No. of players   16 per drill group.

Explanation   A passes to B, B passes behind the wall, and C runs around

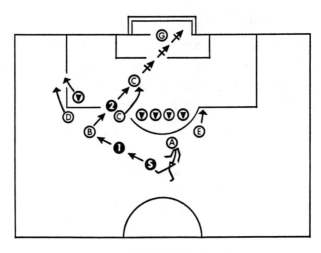

Drill 12–3

Free Kick Drill III

the wall to receive B's pass. C then shoots at the goal. D, F, and G are used to keep defenders out of the play area. All other offensive players should line up away from the main area of play concentration.

Purpose   In this drill, players are positioned in such a manner as to keep defenders away from the main area of play.

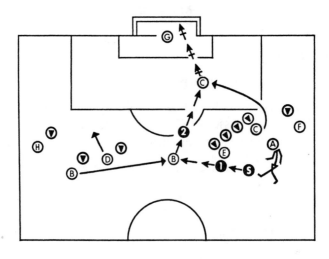

Drill 12–4

Free Kick Drill IV

Drill 12–5   Free Kick Drill V.

No. of players   9 per drill group.

Explanation   A runs as if he is going to kick the ball straight ahead to player D, but instead kicks the ball with the side of his foot to player B. B kicks the ball to C, as seen in the diagram, and C dribbles in for a shot at the goal. C pretends that he is not involved in the play.

Purpose   This drill is designed to make the defense believe that the ball will go to player D, but the direction of the play is reversed and kicked to player C.

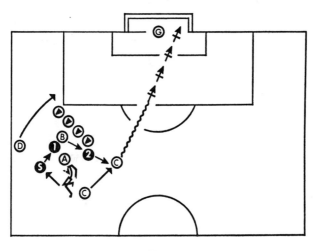

Drill 12–5

Free Kick Drill V

Drill 12–6   Free Kick Drill VI.

No. of players   11 per drill group.

Explanation   A passes through B's legs, and C receives the ball and shoots at the goal.

Purpose   This drill is designed to make the defense believe that the ball will be kicked from B to D. In reality B permits the ball to go through his legs, and C comes from the rear for a shot on goal.

Drill 12–7   Free Kick Drill VII.

No. of players   13 per drill group.

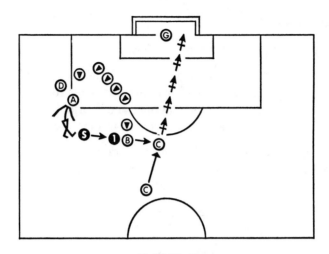

Drill 12–6

Free Kick Drill VI

Explanation A chips the ball over the wall. B and C make crisscross runs to a position behind the wall. All other players break toward the goal. Timing is important: A chips the ball just after B and C start their run.

Purpose In this drill, the ball is chipped over the wall. Players B and C crisscross to confuse the defense.

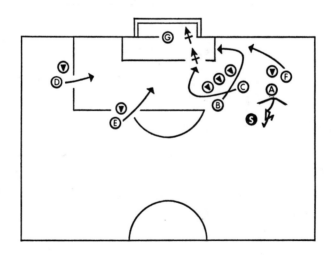

Drill 12–7

Free Kick Drill VII

Drill 12–8   Free Kick Drill VIII.

No. of players   12 per drill group.

Explanation   B runs at the ball as if he is going to kick it to player D. Instead, he steps over the ball and continues his run, yelling for the ball. A then kicks the ball to player C. C shoots at the goal. All other players break toward the goal.

Purpose   Players attempt to deceive the defense into thinking that the play will go to the left side of the wall, but it is immediately reversed and goes around the right side of the wall.

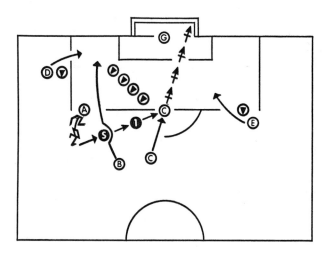

Drill 12–8

Free Kick Drill VIII

Drill 12–9   Goal Kick Drill

No. of players   3 per drill group.

Distance   A to the defensive player—5 to 10 yards.

Explanation   The goalkeeper fakes a kick down the field, then throws the ball outside the penalty area to player A. A immediately kicks the ball back into the penalty area to the goalkeeper, who starts a new attack. To add more pressure on the goalkeeper and player A, move the defensive player closer to player A.

Purpose   According to the rules of the game, the goalkeeper or any other player who takes the kick is not allowed to touch the ball a second time, until it has been touched by another player and has traveled outside the penalty area. In this drill, the ball travels outside the penalty area, is touched by another player, and kicked back into the penalty area. Then the goalkeeper can pick up the ball and start a new attack. This procedure can accomplish two things: it can enable the goalkeeper to start another attack or it can be used to relieve the pressure on player A caused by the close or tight marking of the defensive player.

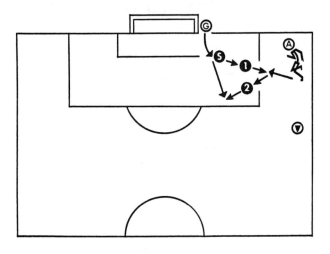

Drill 12–9

Goal Kick Drill

Chapter Thirteen

Relating Kickoff Drills to Match Play

Each special situation or restart is treated in a different manner because the circumstances surrounding each are different. This is so because the defensive positions or line-up of the opponents is different in each case. The rules of the game dictate how these situations should be handled.

Kickoff plays rarely produce the ultimate, a score, because the rules state that each team must remain on its own half of the field until the ball is kicked forward and rolls its circumference. This means that the attacking team must penetrate the entire defense to get an opportunity for a shot on goal. For this reason, many teams pass the ball back into their own half of the field so that the forwards can get enough time to penetrate the other half of the field.

This procedure has another purpose. It causes the defenders to be drawn toward the ball, making a penetration pass possible in the open space or in the space that was vacated by the defenders. Decoy and diagonal runs are used in conjunction with the back pass, to entice defenders to move out of position so that further open space may be created.

Immediately before the kickoff, the attacking players should survey the opponents to see where they are the most vulnerable. If, at this time, obvious weaknesses are seen in the defensive arrangement, attackers should set out to exploit these weaknesses.

If, on the other hand, the opponents provide for depth, width, and balance in their defensive arrangement, they must be drawn out of position in some way. A back pass, a diagonal run, or a decoy run is used to accomplish this.

In defending against a kickoff, most teams stack and protect against an attack down the middle, and permit activity out near the touchlines. For this reason, it makes sense for attackers to use this outside space to achieve penetration by getting the ball out to the wing area. Bringing the ball down the touchlines serves another purpose. It draws the defenders out and sometimes opens the middle of the field for an attack.

Drill 13–1   Kickoff Drill I.

No. of players   6 per drill group.

Explanation   A passes diagonally to player F. C, A, and B make diagonal runs to the right. E runs down the right wing to receive a pass from F. E passes across the field to the other wing player, D, who shoots at the goal. If C, A, or B gets a chance to shoot at the goal, he should attempt it.

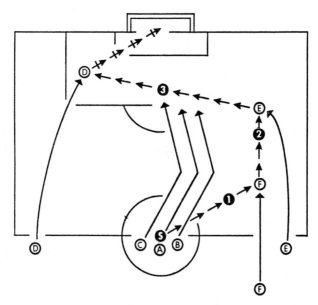

Drill 13–1

Kick-off Drill I

Purpose   In this drill, players create scoring opportunity from a kickoff by drawing players to the right side of the field and quickly switching the play to the left side of the field.

Drill 13–2   Kickoff Drill II.

No. of players   5 per drill group.

Explanation   A pushes a short pass to B. B passes across the field to player D, who dribbles down the field toward the corner of the 18-yard line. Players A, B, and E run down the right side of the field toward the corner of the 18-yard line. Player D either crosses to players A, B, and E or shoots at the goal. D can also pass back to player C.

Purpose   In this drill, players create scoring opportunities from the kick-off by using the following three options: crossing to A, B, or E; D shooting at the goal; or D passing the ball back to C, who shoots at the goal.

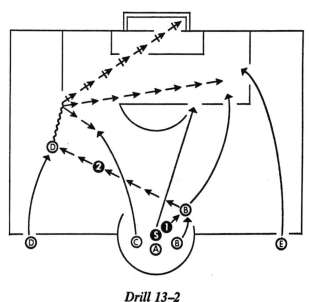

Drill 13–2

Kick-off Drill II

Drill 13–3   Kickoff Drill III.

No. of players   6 per drill group.

Explanation   A passes forward to player B. B passes back to D, who delays his pass till all players have a chance to get down the field. D then kicks the ball into the area where A, C, and E are located. The player who gets control of the ball crosses to player E, who shoots at the goal.

Purpose   The objective of this drill is to draw the defenders to the left side of the field and quickly cross the ball to the right side of the field.

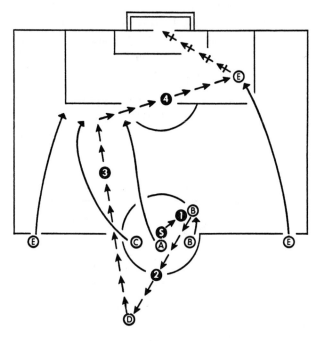

Drill 13–3

Kick-off Drill III

Drill 13–4   Kickoff Drill IV.

No. of players   16 per drill group.

Explanation   Player A makes a short pass to player B. C makes a diagonal run and receives a pass from B. D and E run straight down the field and cut into the center of the field, as shown on the diagram. C dribbles straight ahead and passes off to D or E, depending upon the position of the defenders at that time.

Purpose This drill is used to exploit the space behind the defense by drawing defenders out to guard player C.

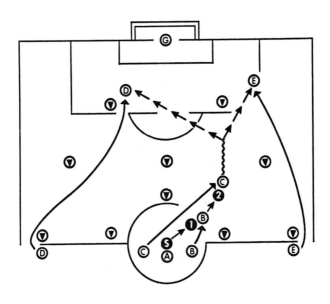

Drill 13–4

Kick-off Drill IV

Drill 13–5 Kickoff Drill V.

No. of players 17 per drill group.

Explanation A passes forward to B, B passes back to F, and F dribbles and passes through to E. E dribbles straight at the defender, veers off to the right and quickly crosses the ball to the space behind the middle defender. Player C moves to the space and the ball, and takes a shot at the goal. A and D make decoy runs.

Purpose From the kickoff, players exploit the space behind the defenders.

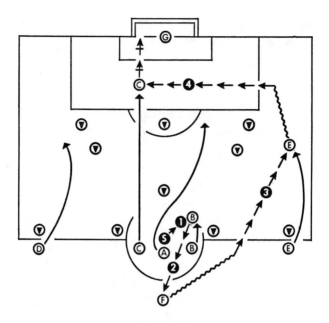

Drill 13–5

Kick-off Drill V

Section Four

Training

To be an effective soccer player, an individual needs three major physical attributes: strength, speed, and endurance. Other qualities such as agility, coordination, flexibility, balance, accuracy and reaction time should not be overlooked in a soccer training program, but the major training emphasis should be to improve strength, speed and endurance. In fact, the developmental range for improvement of these qualities in an individual is greater than the developmental possibilities for improving any other of his physical qualities.

Through a varied and vigorous training program for endurance, speed, and strength, players are able to function at a higher level, with greater speed, and with less signs of fatigue. In general, fatigue interferes with coordination, and causes a decrease in an individual's ability to perform patterns of movement.

Research tells us that muscular power and speed are closely related. In order to run quickly, a player needs muscular strength so that he can move his legs quickly and forcefully. Larson and Yocom say, "Muscular strength and speed can be considered, if so desired, together."[1]

It is a fact that to increase strength, some type of overload-resistance exercise is necessary. The following four methods are commonly used to increase strength:

[1]Lenard A. Larson and Rachael Yocom, *Measurement and Evaluation in Physical Health and Recreation Education* (St. Louis: C.V. Mosby Co., 1951), p. 161.

1. Calisthenic exercises: push-ups, pull-ups, running, etc.
2. Isotonic exercises: Weight training
3. Isometric exercises: Exertion against an immovable object.
4. Combination of Isometric and Isotonic exercises: Using an Exer-geni—Contract muscles against an immovable object for a period of seconds, and then exercise the muscle through its range of motion isotonically.

Each of these methods uses some type of resistance and overload principle to improve an individual's strength. Each has its particular effectiveness in improving strength. Therefore, I suggest using each of the four methods to improve the physical ability of players.

Players must be able to endure the demands of vigorous play for a period of 90 minutes or more without becoming exhausted. Through aerobic and anaerobic fitness programs, players can improve their ability to endure the stresses and strains of the game. Also, their ability to recover from fatigue due to the removal of its byproducts such as lactic acid, etc. is hastened, enabling individuals to perform at higher levels of efficiency.

In aerobic training, players run continually for long periods of time to improve their stamina. In anaerobic training, players run short distances to simultaneously develop speed of movement and stamina.

The aerobic training prepares players to cope with the duration of the game, namely 90 minutes. The anaerobic training prepares players to cope with the various short-distance bursts of speed needed periodically during a game. The training session should use both the aerobic and anaerobic methods of improving fitness, because the physical demands of the game require efficiency in both of these types of physical exertion.

Chapter Fourteen

Training Games

Training games are activities which focus and concentrate on various phases of soccer. The small-sided games (3 to 6 players per team) provide a setting in which the individuals involved receive more frequent encounters than they would normally receive in a full-team scrimmage. Each player touches the ball more times, and each player is confronted frequently with tactical encounters.

The three areas of technique, tactics, and physical conditioning needed to prepare a team for match play are brought together in a mini-setting reflecting the action of match play. The technique and tactic drills in this book are worthless unless players are able to spontaneously understand and execute how they are used in small-sided games. Later on, players should be able to carry over this tactical knowledge into a scrimmage or match play.

Variations are added to these small-sided games to emphasize certain phases of technique and certain tactics that might otherwise be overlooked, for example; playing with the left foot only, two-touch passing, and so forth. These variations, when included in a small-sided game, can be used to concentrate on specifics that you feel need improvement and reinforcement.

The closer the similarity between training and the actual mechanics of the skill used in match play, the better the results. Morehouse and Rouch state that the carryover training for one event will have little or no value for another event. They call this principle "specificity."[1] This principle can be demonstrated by the stiffness that athletes experience when they make the transfer from a sport like soccer to one like basketball. This may be due to the stresses or demands which different sports place upon different muscles. Because the small-sided games provide the experiences and action which closely relate to those which players encounter in match play, this form of training is valuable as far as the principle of specificity is concerned.

Drill 14–1   No Man's Land

No. of players   16 per game.

Equipment   4 flags or cones to mark off 2 goals on each end of half the field.

Explanation   Players must stay on their own third of the field. "No Man's Land" is the middle third of the field, and players cannot enter this section. There are 2 teams—Team A and Team B. Team A has 4 offensive players on one side of the field and 4 defensive players on the other side of the field. Team B has the same arrangement. Play is started when the coach throws the ball to either side of the field. When a defensive

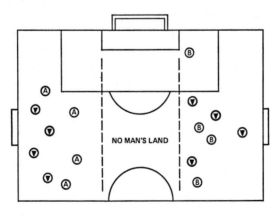

Drill 14–1

No Man's Land

[1]Laurence E. Morehouse and Philip J. Rouch, *Scientific Basis for Athletic Training* (Philadelphia: W.B. Saunders Company, 1958), p. 29.

player gets control of a ball, he tries to pass it to the other side of the field. Offensive players try to score on the small goals at each end of the field. If the ball goes out of bounds, it is restarted by a throw-in. After a goal is scored, play is started again when the coach throws a ball to the side of the field opposite from where the goal was scored.

Purpose In a confined area, players practice all the skills involved in the game of soccer without mid-field build-up.

Variation Use 2 soccer balls to pick up the speed of the game.

Drill 14–2 Either Side

No. of players 9 per game.

Equipment 2 flags or cones to mark off a goal.

Explanation Scoring may occur from either side of the goal, in the middle of the field. The defensive team uses man-for-man marking, and the offensive team may score through the goals. If the defensive team intercepts the ball, they try to make 5 consecutive passes, which constitute a score. After a score, play is started again by a ball dropped in the penalty area.

Purpose The defensive players practice breaking away from the conjested area of play. Offensive players practice quick shooting.

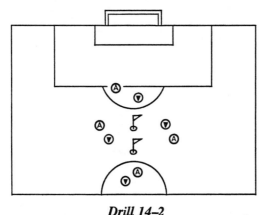

Drill 14–2

Either Side

Drill 14–3 Clearing

No. of players 14 to 22 per game.

Equipment   8 soccer balls.

Explanation   The objective of this game is to get all 8 soccer balls on the other side of the field. Players must kick to the other side of the field without hesitation. Defensive player A and offensive player A start the game by rapidly kicking all four balls to the other side of the field.

Purpose   Players practice quick clearing and long kicking.

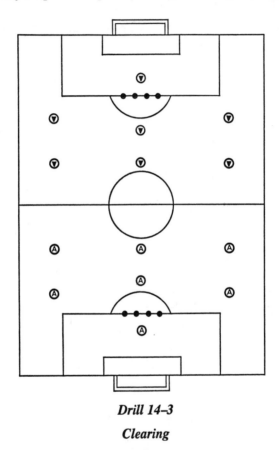

Drill 14–3

Clearing

Drill 14–4   Hit Me (No Diagram)

No. of players   14 to 20 in the penalty area, and 7 to 10 if playing in the center circle.

Equipment   Every other player has a ball.

Explanation   Each offensive player has a ball. The game is played with two teams inside the penalty area or inside the center circle. One team tries to hit the other team players with the ball below waist level. Play is continued till all defensive players have been hit with a ball.

Caution: No wild kicking is permitted.

Purpose This drill is used to improve players' physical fitness and agility. It is also a good change of pace from the regular practice routine.

Drill 14–5 Flag Knock-Down

No. of players 10—2 teams of 5 players.

Equipment 8 Flags

Explanation The objective of this game is to knock over the opponents' 4 flags. Each team uses two defensive players to protect their flags while the other three players attack the opposition's flags. When the ball is on the opposing half of the field, the defenders act as support players for the attack. The three offensive players on each team are the only players permitted to knock over the flags.

Purpose In this drill, offensive players practice accurate shooting. The defensive players practice defensive skills while they protect the flags. Defensive players also practice supporting the attack.

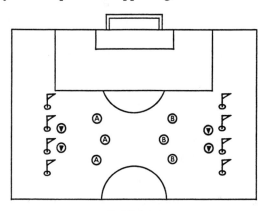

Drill 14–5

Flag Knock Down

Drill 14—6 Half-Field (6 On 6)—No Goals—Two Goals—Four Goals (No Diagram)

No. of players 12 per game.

Equipment 4 small goals, or 8 cones or flags.

Explanation A regular game of soccer is played on half of the field: first, with no goals; second, with 2 goals; third, with 4 goals. Each of these variations can be played for about 5 minutes each, depending upon the physical conditioning of the players.

Purpose   These small-sided games provide a setting for more players to take part in the action of the game. In the "No Goal" game, players concentrate on their passing and ball control skills.

In the "2 Goal" game, players get a chance to play and participate more in the game's action due to field's size and the number of players.

The purpose of the "4 Goal" game is to provide a setting for frequent switching of the play to less crowded areas of the field.

Drill 14–7   Three Team Soccer (No Diagram)

No. of players   9 per game.

Equipment   6 flags or cones to mark off 3 goals, three different sets of colored shirts.

Explanation   Three teams play soccer on half the soccer field. Each team is assigned a goal. The 2 teams without the ball play against the team with the ball. Play is started when the coach throws a ball into the middle of the field.

Purpose   In this game, players practice all the skills in the entire game of soccer. Quick role changes from offense to defense are seen in this drill.

Drill 14–8   Two Ball Soccer Five-on-Five (No Diagram)

No. of players   10 per game.

Explanation   A regular game of soccer is played on half the field, and only two balls are in play at all times. After a goal is scored, play is started again when the coach quickly throws another ball into the middle of the field. If a ball goes out of bounds it is restarted by a throw-in.

Purpose   The direction of play changes frequently in this game; consequently, players are constantly attacking, defending, counter attacking, and reorganizing.

Drill 14–9   Three Passers and One Shooter

No. of players   9 per game.

Equipment   4 flags or cones to set aside one-fourth of the field.

Explanation   The coach designates one player to be a shooter, (A), who is the only offensive player permitted to shoot at the goal. All other players are passers, (B). The shooter must get free from the defensive players to get a shot at the goal. The passers must tease the defenders out of position so that the shooter can get behind them.

Purpose Instead of forcing the ball through the defense, offensive players learn to make the defensive players come out after the ball.

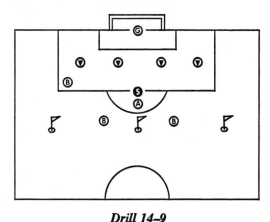

Drill 14–9

3 Passers and 1 Shooter

Drill 14–10 Ball Possession Five-on-Five (No Diagram)

No. of players 10 per game.

Equipment 2 clocks.

Explanation Play is on half the field. The length of each team's possession of the ball is timed. Team A's clock is running while team A is in possession of the ball. If team A loses possession, team A's clock is stopped, and team B's clock is started. The first team to accumulate five minutes' possession time is declared the winner.

Purpose Players practice ball-possession skills, which are an important element of the game of soccer and of team play.

Drill 14–11 Four Zone Passing Soccer

No. of players 12 per game.

Equipment 9 flags or cones.

Distance Divide the field into 4 equal zones with the flags or cones.

Explanation Each player must stay in his designated zone. Players try to pass through a zone without an interception. When a ball is intercepted, play continues with the opponents attempting to pass through a zone. Players may pass a ball to another player within a zone, in order to set up a safe pass to a player in another zone.

Purpose   Players practice passing and receiving a ball with control and accuracy.

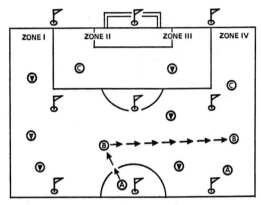

Drill 14–11

4 Zone Passing Soccer

Drill 14–12   Mid-Field Build-Up

No. of players   9 per game.

Distance   Divide the field into 3 zones from end line to end line.

Equipment   10 cones or flags to mark off the three zones.

Explanation   Team B starts the play against Team A. Team B tries to penetrate team A and score a goal. If team A recovers the ball, the players ᶜhould attempt to get back into the neutral zone and proceed to set up an attack against team C. If team C intercepts the ball, they proceed to the neutral zone and set up an attack against team B. Players cannot challenge the other team in the neutral zone. The final objective is to get a shot on goal.

Purpose   This drill helps a team to develop mid-field confidence.

Drill 14–13   No-Pass Soccer (No Diagram)

No. of players   10 per game. (5 per team)

Equipment   2 small goals and 2 soccer balls.

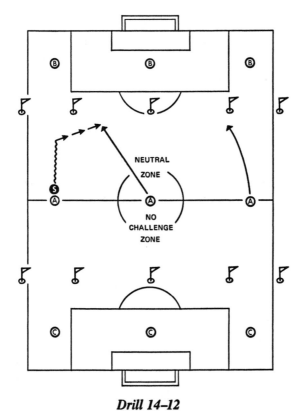

Drill 14–12

Mid-Field Buildup

Explanation This game is played on half the playing field. Play is started when the coach throws two balls onto the playing field. Players must dribble the ball till they are tackled. Players are not permitted to pass the ball to anyone, and they attempt to dribble and score a goal. When a dribbler loses a ball, he immediately tries to get one back from the opposition.

Purpose The purpose of this game is to promote dribbling and tackling skills.

Drill 14–14   No-Retreat Dribble.

No. of players   5 per drill group.

Equipment   18 cones or flags.

Explanation   The field is divided in half, lengthwise. Next, the field is divided into four hostile zones and four neutral zones, as seen in the diagram. Players attempt to dribble through a hostile zone to a neutral zone. Defense players must stay in the hostile zone. When an offensive player loses his ball to the defensive player, the play is stopped and the offensive player takes his ball and moves to the next neutral zone and starts a new attack. If an offensive player successfully dribbles through a hostile zone, he receives one point; and if he fails, he moves on to the next zone without a point. Once a player moves into a hostile zone, he must move forward; he cannot retreat back to a previously used neutral zone.

If a defensive player forces an offensive player out of bounds, the offensive player moves to the next neutral zone without a point.

Purpose   Offensive players practice dribbling and feinting skills. Defensive players practice tackling skills.

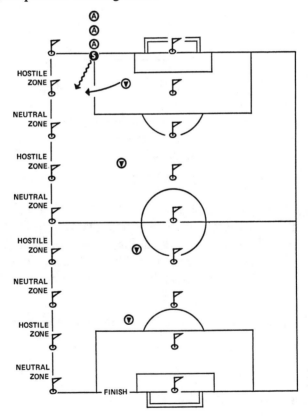

Drill 14–14

No Retreat Dribble

Scoring 4 points—super, 3 points—excellent, 2 points—good, 1 point—practice needed, 0 points—next time.

Drill 14–15 Dribble and Back Pass—Five-on-Five (No Diagram)

Equipment 4 cones to mark off the 2 goals.

Explanation Play takes place on half the field. Players can only move the ball forward by dribbling. Back passes are permitted, but no passes forward toward the goal are allowed.

Purpose Players practice dribbling skills and getting into position to make a back pass.

Drill 14–16 Two Teams Against the Goalkeeper (No Diagram)

No. of players 9 per drill group.

Area of Play Penalty area.

Explanation Two teams play the game of soccer in the penalty area. Either team can score. The coach throws the ball in the penalty area to start the game. Teams should use "One-touch" passing and shooting. When the ball goes out of the penalty area, play is started again with a throw-in. Offsides are permitted. When a team has possession of the ball, the other team tries to prevent a score. The goalkeeper is the only permanent defender.

Purpose The primary purpose is for players to practice quick shooting at the goal. The secondary purpose is to give the goalkeeper practice in a game where there is frequent shooting.

Drill 14–17 Rebound Soccer (No Diagram)

No. of players 10 per game.

Equipment 2 benches or boards.

Explanation Benches or any rebound surface are used for goals. Play is continuous unless the ball goes out of bounds. Goals are scored by hitting the benches or rebound surface. When a ball rebounds off the bench after a score, a player can score again by an immediate shot at the same goal.

Purpose Players practice following up their shots. This is a good drill for improving the physical condition of the players because the play is continuous.

Drill 14–18   Four Goal—Dual Scoring

No. of players   10 per game. Five-on-Five

Equipment   8 flags or cones.

Explanation   There are two ways to score goals: first, by kicking the ball through the front of the goal; second, by completing five consecutive passes. Play is continuous unless the ball crosses the boundary lines. If a ball goes out of bounds, it is restarted by a throw-in. When players are attacking a goal and the area of the goal becomes crowded, players should quickly switch to another goal and continue the attack.

Purpose   Players practice ball control and related skills. This drill develops the players' ability to quickly switch play to less crowded areas of the field.

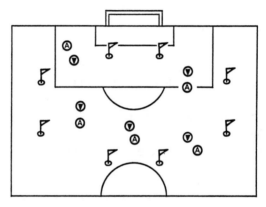

Drill 14–18

4 Goal—Dual Scoring

Drill 14–19   Wing Attack

No. of players   2 full teams.

Equipment   8 flags or cones.

Explanation   Players score by passing the ball into the corner area and then passing it out to a teammate before an opponent gets a chance to touch it. If the ball is touched first by an opponent after it comes out of the corner area, it must go back into the corner area before another score can be made.

Purpose   This drill forces players to work the ball into the corner. Players practice quick switching of the play from one side of the field to the other.

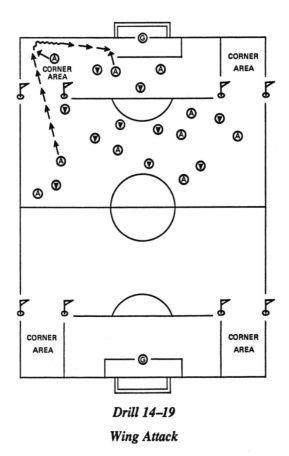

Drill 14–19

Wing Attack

Drill 14–20   Crab Soccer (No Diagram)

No. of players   2 teams of equal number of players.

Equipment   2 small goals, or 4 cones or flags to mark off the goals on half the field.

Explanation   The game is played like a regular game of soccer, except that play is in a crab position. In other words, players place their hands and feet on the ground with their stomach facing the sky. The ball is played with the feet. No goalkeepers are used.

Purpose   This is a physical conditioning drill to improve upper-body strength.

Drill 14–21   Horseback Soccer (No Diagram)

No. of players   2 teams of equal number of players.

Equipment   2 small goals, or 4 cones or flags to mark off the goals on half the field.

Explanation   The game is played like a regular game of soccer with the following exceptions: each player has a partner who rides on his shoulders in a horse and rider arrangement; the game is played with no goalkeepers; no physical contact is permitted; and after each minute of play, the coach blows a whistle and the players change positions. The horse becomes the rider and the rider becomes the horse. This is done because the game is very strenuous.

Purpose   This is an overload-training game to improve strength in the legs, back, and neck.

Chapter Fifteen

Training Activities with a Ball

This chapter includes activities to improve ball-handling technique. Also, in the latter section of this chapter, you will find competitive conditioning relay games.

With the exception of the relay contest and the pressure training drills, the ball-handling activities can be performed by a person alone, indoors or outdoors. All that is needed is a ball and a small space to practice in. Off season, these individual activities can be used to keep players tuned to the feel of the ball, and to maintain a level of confidence in handling the ball. Further, these activities can prevent monotony from creeping into the daily practice routine.

Through these exercises a player can improve his control over the ball: he can develop the ability to make it go where he wants it to go.

The competitive conditioning relay games are used to build individual skill and, at the same time, to build speed and stamina. An economical training program that combines the physical fitness aspect of a game and the technical skills necessary to play soccer is called pressure training.

Pressure training is used to improve endurance and to improve the ability of a muscle and muscle groups to contract repeatedly. In one drill, soccer balls are served in a rapid fire fashion to a player who returns the balls as quickly as he receives them. This procedure is continued for a period of 40 to 45 seconds.

Pressure-training exercises can be developed for every technique, including head, passing, receiving, controlling, and tackling. An example of a heading pressure-training exercise involves the formation of a 10-yard square by four players. A fifth player stands in the center of the square. Each player at the square's corner has a ball in his hands, and each, in his turn, throws his ball to the player in the middle of the square. The player in the middle heads the ball and returns it to the player of the square's corner. This procedure is repeated by the other players at the corners of the square, each throwing his ball in turn. As soon as the player in the center heads the ball back, the next ball should be on its way in order to keep the pressure on him.

Throughout various chapters in this book you will find many other drills that can be modified and used as pressure-training drills.

Any overload conditioning program should be geared to the age level, physical maturity, and exerience of the group involved. The intensity of these conditioning programs should be increased as the players' readiness for this type of training develops.

Drill 15–1   Individual Training Activities with a Ball

A. Jump over a series of balls or cones while dribbling a ball alongside the cones or balls. The balls or cones are placed five yards apart.

B. Bounce a ball with the sole of the foot while hopping on the other foot.

C. Juggle a ball with the instep, inside of the foot, outside of the foot, thigh, head. Develop combinations of these juggling skills.

D. With the ball between the heels of the feet, jump up into the air and flick the ball over the back of your head. The ball should land in front of you.

E. Throw a ball in front of you, let it bounce, and kick it back over your head. Let it bounce again, kick it back over your head again, and so on.

F. Throw a ball into the air, perform a forward roll, and trap the ball before it hits the ground.

G. Put a ball on the ground in front of you. Pull it toward you with your feet. Place your toe under it, and flick it up into the air. Kick the ball over your head, turn, and trap the ball with the sole of the foot and repeat.

H. Clamp the ball with the Achilles' tendon of the left leg and with the inside of the right toe; flip the ball back over your shoulders with the left heel.

I. Throw a ball over your shoulder; kick it back over your shoulder with the outside of the foot.

J. Kick against a wall or the corner of a room:

   a. Standing about 10 feet away from a wall, throw a ball high on the wall, about 10 feet high. When it rebounds, tap it or juggle it with your right foot, then volley-kick it back to the wall with your left foot.

Variation Repeat the same drill using the opposite foot.

   b. Same procedure as "a," only tap or juggle the ball with your thigh, let it drop to your feet, and then volley-kick it back to the wall with your left foot. Do this before the ball hits the ground.

Variation On the rebound, trap the ball on one thigh, then tap it to the other thigh. Let it drop to the feet, and volley-kick it back to the wall.

   c. Same as "a," only first trap the ball with the chest, let it drop to the feet, then kick it back to the wall before it hits the ground.

   d. Same as "a," only the ball on the rebound goes from the thigh to the foot and is headed back to the wall.

   e. Same as "a," only the ball on the rebound goes from the thigh to the foot. When the ball rebounds off the foot, kick it high into the air, then turn 180 degrees and kick it back over your head to the wall.

   f. Same as "a," only the ball on the rebound goes from the head, to the thigh, to the foot.

   g. Practice any combination of "a" through "f."

   Using the corner of the gymnasium, first pass to one wall, then on the rebound, pass to the other wall with the other foot. Vary the distance you stand away from the wall.

Variation Use two balls. While one ball is rebounding off the wall, kick the other ball against the other wall.

Kick and head a soccer ball in a four wall handball court. Try to kick or head the ball before it hits the floor three times.

Variation   Play a game of handball using a soccer ball and your feet. The ball must be kicked before it hits the floor three times.

Dribble a ball randomly while blindfolded. Another player should be assigned to watch over you for safety purposes.

Drill 15–2   Leave It (No Diagram)

No. of players   As many as will fit on the end line.

Equipment   1 ball per player.

Explanation   Each player has a ball. Play is started by a whistle. Each player dribbles his ball to the first station and leaves his ball on the station line. He then sprints back to touch the starting line. After touching the starting line, he sprints back, gets his ball and dribbles it to the second station. Once again he leaves it and sprints back to the end line, and so on to the third station.

Purpose   The purpose of this drill is to improve physical endurance. Players cover over 500 yards in this drill.

Drill 15–3   Hit the Post Relay

No. of players   2 teams of equal number.

Explanation   Player A from team I and player A from team II start the relay race by dribbling to the other end of the field, first hitting one of the goalposts with the ball, then hitting the other. They then dribble to the opposite end of the field and pass the ball to player B who continues the relay, and so on. Players must successfully hit each post before they continue to the next phase of the relay race.

Purpose   Players improve their speed while dribbling a ball. They also improve their physical conditioning.

Drill 15–4   Cross-Over Relay

No. of players   4 teams of equal number.

Equipment   4 sets of 8 different colored shirts.

Explanation   Players line up as indicated on the diagram. On a whistle signal, players dribble across to the other end of the field, and pass off to

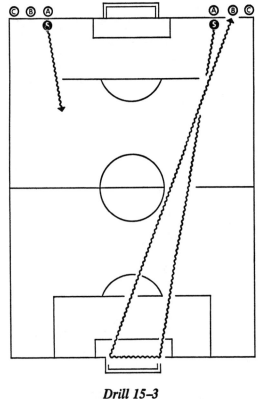

Drill 15–3

Hit the Post Relay

a player with the same letter: A to A, B to B, etc. Players cannot pass off until they reach the 18-yard line on the other side of the field. The relay then continues.

Purpose   Players improve their physical conditioning and their speed in dribbling a ball.

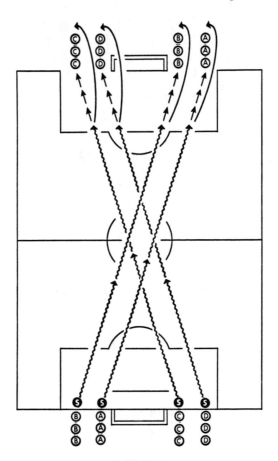

Drill 15–4

Cross Over Relay

Chapter Sixteen

General Conditioning Exercises Without a Ball

STARTING POSITIONS

Standing
Sitting
Kneeling
Lying

Standing

Arm Circles   Extend arms out to the side; rotate in wide circles, both clockwise and counter clockwise.

Straddle jumps   Bounce on the balls of the feet three or four times and leap straight up. Touch the toes with the hands out to the sides. Legs should be straight.

Chest Stretcher   Arms straight out in front, parallel to the ground; then extend them out and back.

Tuck Jump   Bounce on the balls of the feet three or four times. Leap up and touch the knees with the hands. Momentarily, at the peak of the leap, bend at the knee and at the hip joint. Land on your feet and repeat the procedure.

Leg Circles   While standing on one foot, circle the other leg. Repeat this exercise while standing on the other foot.

Lunge   Lunge right to the count of three. Lunge left to the count of three.

Run in Place   Knees high.

Toe Raise   Raise up on the toes, stretching the arms over the head.

Hop on One Foot   First the left, then the right.

Head Circling   First to the right, then to the left.

Trunk Bending and Back Bending   Bend forward and touch the toes, keeping the legs straight, straighten the body, then bend backward.

Straight Leg Raise   Standing on the left foot, raise the right leg forward until it is parallel with the ground. Keep both legs as straight as possible. Repeat, standing on the left foot.
Variation: Lift the leg back, instead of forward.

Straight Leg Side Raise   Standing on the left foot, raise the right leg away from the body to the side. Standing on the right foot, repeat the same with the left foot. Alternate straight leg side raises.

Gate   Standing on one foot, draw the other knee up in front with the upper leg parallel to the ground. In this position, move the knee out to the side and back again. Alternate to the other leg.

Foot and Ankle Exercises   Rock up on the toes, rock back down on the heels. Walk on the insides of the feet. Walk on the outside of the feet.

Side Twisting   Standing with the arms extended away from the sides, turn from the waist, twisting first to the right, then to the left.

Piked Chest Expander   Bend forward at the waist till the upper body is parallel with the ground. Let the arms hang straight down. Remain in this position and raise the arms out and back. Lower the arms back to the starting position and repeat.

Circle Upper Body   Place the hands behind the head. In this position circle the upper body left, forward, and to the right.

Alternate Toe Touch   From a straddle standing position, bend forward at the waist (keep the legs straight), and touch both hands on the right foot. Return to the starting position and repeat this procedure, touching the left foot.

Pantomime Heading Exercises   Without a ball, pretend that you are heading a ball. In between each exercise, bounce two or three times on the balls of the feet.

Sitting

Knees to Chest First, raise the left knee to the chest, then the right knee, then both. The hands are behind you on the ground.

Straight Leg Raise Lift the right leg, first, then the left leg, then both. Keep the legs straight. The hands are behind you on the ground.

Sit-Up Series (ten repetitions of each exercise)

a. *Bent-knee Sit-Up*

b. *Sitting Twist* With the hands behind your head and the knees bent, twist your upper body till your right elbow touches your left knee. Repeat the same procedure with your left elbow touching your right knee.

c. *One-forth Sit-Up* In a back-lying and bent-knee position, curl the upper body (chin on the chest) and perform a quarter of a bent-knee sit-up.

d. *Hip Raise* In a back-lying position, raise the feet until they are on the ground over the head. Bring them back to the original position and repeat the exercise.

Kneeling

Chest to Knees With the buttocks close to the ground, bend forward and place the chest on the knees and back to the original starting position. The hands are behind the back.

One Knee to the Chest Balancing on one knee, bring the other knee to the chest and back to the ground again. Repeat balancing on the other knee.

Lying (prone position)

Push-up and Clap the Hands

Head and Upper Body Raise Keep the hips on the ground and arch the back. Hold for three seconds and return to the original starting position.

Raise Opposite Arm and Leg Repeat using the other leg and the other arm.

Push-up and Half Circle From a push-up position, half circle the legs around one arm, lay back—roll over—push-up and repeat going to the other side.

Lame Duck   In a push-up starting position, raise one leg back and up. Proceed to move forward then to twenty yards in this position.

Lying (supine position)

Piked Sit-ups and Toe Touch   Bend forward at the waist, straighten legs and touch the hands and feet together in the air.

Back Arch   Place the palms of the hands on the ground behind your head. Bend the knees and place the bottoms of the feet on the ground. From this position, push up into an arch and hold for six seconds.

Half Leg Raise   Both legs straight and together. Raise both legs off the ground and hold for six seconds and repeat.

Leg Raise   Arms straight out. Bring the left foot up to touch the right hand and repeat this procedure touching the right foot to the left hand.

Shoulder Stand   Roll the lower body backward and upward; place the hands on the hips. Hold this position for six seconds.

Neck Bridge   Same as the back arch bend, only the weight is on the head and on the bottoms of the feet. Rock back and forth in this position.

Feet Over the Head and Straight Leg Sit-ups   Straighten legs. Roll the lower body over the head until the feet touch the ground. Lower the feet to the starting position, and perform a straight leg sit-up. Repeat the entire procedure.

Drill 16–1   Four Stations

No. of players   unlimited

Equipment   10 flags or cones to mark off the stations.

Explanation   Players run to the first line, perform ten push-ups, then sprint back to the starting line. Next players run to the second line, perform ten bent-knee sit-ups, sprint back to the starting line, and so on. Each player covers over 400 yards.

Purpose   Players develop and improve their physical conditioning.

Drill 16–2   Sprint to the Front

No. of players   6 per group.

Explanation   Players jog around the field in groups of six. The last player in line sprints to the front of the line.

Purpose   Players improve their physical conditioning.

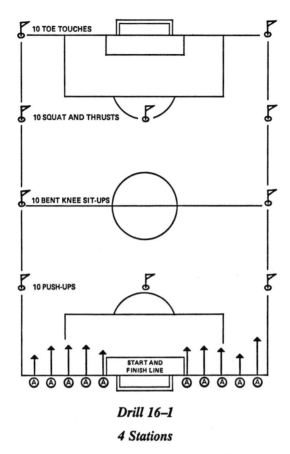

10 TOE TOUCHES

10 SQUAT AND THRUSTS

10 BENT KNEE SIT-UPS

10 PUSH-UPS

START AND
FINISH LINE

Drill 16–1

4 Stations

Variation   Players dribble a soccer ball when performing this exercise.

Drill 16–3   200-Yard Plus Relay

No. of players   4 teams of equal number.

Explanation   C and D, on the right side of the field, run around the left side of the far goal. A and B, starting on the left side of the field, run around the right side of the goal. This is a relay race in which players race over 200 yards.

Purpose   Players improve their physical conditioning.

Variation   Players can dribble a ball in performing this relay race.

Other Running and Conditioning Exercises
for Endurance and Speed

A. Running 100-yard sprints:

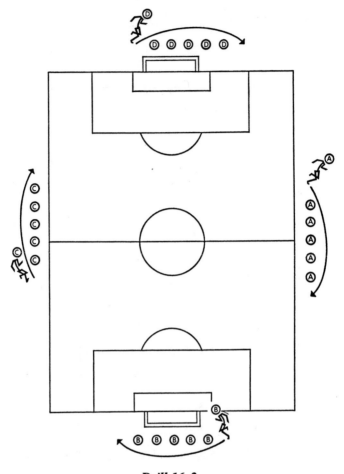

Drill 16–2

Sprint to the Front

    a. Regular running style

    b. Running backward

    c. Running sideward

    d. Skipping

B. Running up hills or stairs.

C. Running through wooded areas.

D. Running and stopping on a whistle signal.

E. Alternating jogging and sprinting. All participants jog until the coach blows a whistle. On the whistle, participants sprint until they hear the next whistle and then they jog again.

F. Changing direction—Players follow hand signals given by the

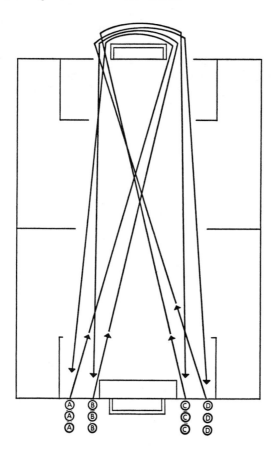

Drill 16–3

200 Yard Plus Relay

coach. If the coach points to the right, players run to the right. If the coach points back, the players run backward, and so on.

G. Players run down the field. When the coach blows the whistle, players jump high, as if they are heading a ball. Then they run again and repeat the same procedure when they hear the whistle again.

H. Place cones ten yards apart all the way down the field. Players run and jump over the cones.

I. Players run down the field. When the coach blows a whistle, players stop, do a forward roll, get back to their feet, and run again until the next whistle. This procedure is repeated down the field.

J. Horse and rider race for fifty yards. Participants change roles after fifty yards.

K. Two players line one behind the other. On a signal, both players race 100 yards to the other end of the field. The runner in front tries to obstruct the runner in back by staying in front of him while running down the field. The player in front is not allowed to use his hands to obstruct the man behind him. The player in front keeps moving into the pathway of the runner in the back.

Bibliography

Books

Batty, Eric, *Soccer—Coaching the Modern Way,* London: Faber and Faber 1969.

Beim, George, *Principles of Modern Soccer,* Boston: Houghton Mifflin Co., 1977.

Bradley, Gordon and Clive Toye, (eds.) *Playing Soccer the Professional Way,* New York: Harper and Row Publishers, 1973.

Casico, Chuck, *Soccer in the U.S.A.* New York: Robert Luce Inc., 1975.

Csanadi, Arpad, *Soccer,* Vols. I and II, Budapest: Corvina Press Co., 1965; New York: Athenaeum, 1965.

Di Clementi, Frank, Soccer Illustrated for Coach and Player. New York: Ronald Press Co. 1968.

Eastham, George, and Ken Jones, *Soccer Science—How to Play and Win,* Chicago, Quadrangle Books, 1966.

Fox, Edward L., and Donald Mathews, *Interval Training, Conditioning for Sports and General Fitness,* Phila., London, Toronto, W.B. Saunders Co., 1974.

Glanville, Brian, *Soccer,* New York; Crown Publishers Inc., 1968.

Goldman, Howard, *Soccer,* Boston; Allyn Bacon Inc., 1969.

Kirby, George and George Sullivan, *An All-Star Book,* Chicago: Follett Publishing Company, 1971.

Lammich, Gunter and Dr. Heinz Kadow, (eds.) *Warm Up for Soccer,* Chicago: Follett Publishing Co., Inc., 1975.

Larson, Lenard, and Rachael Yocom, *Measurement and Evaluation in Physical, Health, and Recreation Education,* (St. Louis: C.V. Mobsy Company, 1951.)

Liss, Howard, *Soccer, International Game,* New York: Funk and Wagnalls, 1967.

Menendez, Julie, and Matt Boxer, *Soccer,* N.Y. The Ronald Press Co., 1968.

Moffat, Bob, *The Basic Soccer Guide,* Mountain View, California: World Publications, 1975.

Morehouse, Laurence, E. and Philip J. Rosch, *Scientific Basis for Athletic Training,* Phila., W.B. Saunders Co., 1958.

Muse, Bill, and Dan White, *We Can Teach You to Play Soccer,* New York: Hawthorn Books Inc., 1976.

Ruege, Klaus, *Inside Soccer for Beginners,* Chicago: Henry Regnery Co., 1976.

Schmid, Irvin, John McKeon, and Melvin Schmid, (eds.) *Skills and Strategies of Successful Soccer,* Englewood Cliffs, N.J.: Prentice-Hall Inc., 1968.

Timby, Robin, *Soccer Techniques and Tactics,* New York: Arco Publishing Co. Inc., 1973.

Vogelsinger, Hubert, *The Challenge of Soccer,* Boston: Allyn and Bacon, Inc., 1973.

Wade, Allen, *The FA Guide to Training and Coaching,* Toronto, William Heineman Ltd., 1967.

Waters, Earle, Paul Hawk and John Squiers, *Physical Education Series* 3rd Edition, Anapolis, Maryland, U.S. Naval Institute, 1961.

Wilson, Bob, *Goalkeeping,* Pelham Books, 1970.

Periodicals

Barry, Bob, "Functional Training for Fullbacks," *Soccer World,* (January 1976), 24.

Biem, George, "Attacking from the Throw-in," *Scholastic Coach,* (November 1970), 46, 48.

Beim, George, "The Short Corner Kick," *Scholastic Coach,* (September 1970), 48–50.

Chyzowych, Walter, "Basic Tactics," *Soccer World,* (June 1974), 25, 26.

Dikranian, Bob, "Skill Learning in 3 Stages," *Soccer World,* (February 1976), 22–24.

Faust, Jeff, "The Turning Whirl," *Soccer World,* (August 1975), 15.

Gainly, Pat, "The Vaughn Christian Winning Philosophy," *Soccer World,* (October 1975), 18–19.

Lawther, Frederick, "Goal Shotting," Soccer World, (August 1974), 29.

Maher, Alan, "A Word From Holland," *Soccer World,* (January 1976), 14–15.

Maher, Alan, "Don't Fade Away," *Soccer World,* (June 1975), 18–19.

Maher, Alan, "Dutch-Style Passing and Running Soccer Drills," *Scholastic Coach*, (September 1976), 22–23.

Maher, Alan, "Four on Two Drills," *Soccer World*, (August 1975), 18–19.

Maher, Alan, "Learning the Basics of Practice," *Soccer World*, (April 1977), 7–8.

Maher, Alan, "Soccer Practice, English-Grid Style," *Scholastic Coach*, (November 1977), 66, 68, 102.

Maher, Alan, "Swing with Soccer by Going Square," *Soccer World*, April 1975), 10, 11.

Maher, Alan, "Technical Tips," *Soccer World*, (August 1977), 28–29.

Maher, Alan, "The Old One-Two," Soccer World, (June 1976), 10, 11.

Maher, Alan, "The Winning Wing," *Soccer World*, (December 1976), 13.

Maher, Alan, "Three on One Drills," *Soccer World*, (February 1976), 28.

Maisner, Larry, "Rounding Out Those Corner Kicks," *Soccer World*, (May 1977), 20–21.

Moffat, Bobby, "Survival of the Fittest," *Soccer World*, (December 1976), 9.

Musgrove, "Splitting the Defense—Wall Passing," *Soccer World*, (June 1975), 26–27.

Nonbadge, A., "Digging Out the Ball," *Soccer World*, (June 1975), 14–15.

Shults, F. D. "Scoring from the Kick-Off," Scholastic Coach, (September 1970), 7, 116–117.

Vial, Sil, "Beating the Best," *Soccer World*, (April 1974), 22–26.

Viger, Bill, "Circuit Skills," *Soccer World*, (October 1977), 4–6.

Viger, Bill, "Conditioning with the Ball," *Soccer World*, (January 1976), 20–21.

Viger, Bill, "The Conditioning Circuit," *Soccer World*, (October 1975), 21.

Vogelsinger, Hubert, "Game Simulated Soccer Training and Conditioning," *Scholastic Coach*, (September 1970), 96, 99, 110, 112.

Vogelsinger, Hubert, "Practice Organization for Soccer," *Scholastic Coach* (September 1972), 67–68, 70, 75, 108, 109, 114, 1161 118.

Vogelsinger, Hubert "Practice Organization for Soccer," *Scholastic Coach*, (October 1972), 27, 69.

Index